# THE CORNISH FARMER IN AUSTRALIA

## OR

*Australian Adventure:*
*Cornish Colonists and the Expansion*
*of Adelaide and the South*
*Australian Agricultural Frontier*

By
Philip Payton BSc PhD
(Bardic Name—Car Dyvresow)

Published by Dyllansow Truran
Trewolsta, Trewirgie, Redruth, Cornwall

© 1987 Philip Payton BSc PhD

Printed and bound in Great Britain
by A. Wheaton & Co. Ltd, Exeter

ISBN 1 85022 029 8

# THE CORNISH FARMER IN AUSTRALIA
## or
## Australian Adventure:
## Cornish Colonists and the Expansion of Adelaide and the South Australian Agricultural Frontier

*By*
Philip Payton BSc PhD
(Bardic Name: Car Dyvresow)
Foreword by A. L. Rowse

Maps by Elizabeth Yeardley BSc

Dyllansow Truran

For Unity Ceinwen

# Contents

# Foreword

The story of the Cornish Emigration overseas is the most important in the history of our Cornish people. It has been a very individual factor in the building up of new and young nations, notably in the United States, and hardly less significantly in Australia. Nor is their contribution to be neglected in New Zealand, South Africa, Canada and elsewhere.

It has, however, been sadly and unimaginatively overlooked. Wherever they have gone Cornish folk have been content to be good citizens and make their contribution in their new homes, grateful for the wider opportunities and better living it has provided them.

Their contribution has chiefly lain in mining and quarrying of every kind, in the technical and mechanical industries where their gifts have brightly shone. Foremost amongst Cornishmen was the scientist of genius, Sir Humphry Davy. But they have worked in other fields too, in religion and education, as ministers and teachers, in the law and politics, in the Services on land and at sea. Greatest of Australian soldiers, who did a splendid job in both World Wars in our time, was the Cornish Field-Marshal Blamey.

For a number of years I have been anxious to see a book on the Cornish in Australia, which would follow on the lines of *The Cornish in America*, with which I hoped to set a model for other books filling out the story around the world.

At last my lead is being followed up. It is particularly appropriate that we should learn about the Cornish in Australia, when her Prime Minister, Bob Hawke, is a Cornishman by descent on both sides of his family. Nor did his predecessor, Sir Robert Menzies, forget that he was a Cornish Sampson on his mother's side.

Dr Philip Payton has been doing excellent work with his books, mainly on the mining folk in Australia. We appreciate what a wonderful job those fellows did in earlier days in building up that beautiful country. Now Dr Payton, with his gift for research and conscientious investigation, is extending his field into other areas.

No one is more delighted than I am, as a correspondent when young of the famous Sir Langdon Bonython, the newspaper magnate who was generous to both South Australia and to Cornwall—for he kept up his association with the Little Land of his forebears. (Few people realise that the poet Longfellow was a Bonython by descent).

In his new book—fascinating to all of us—Dr Payton shows us how the Cornish folk in South Australia pushed forward the frontiers, not only in mining but in agriculture, into industry, journalism, religion. They were essentially constructive, essentially democratic like the community they came from at home—and so felt at home in the new communities they helped so notably to create.

I am glad that justice is being done to them and their work, in their hard-working lives, at last; and I hope that Dr Payton will go forward to expand his frontiers into other communities and States, until we have a full picture of their brave enterprise in all fields, throughout Australia.

A. L. ROWSE,<br>
Trenarren,<br>
February 1986

# Acknowledgements

It was John Tregenza who, during my earliest days as a postgraduate student at the University of Adelaide, emphasised that the common view that all nineteenth-century Cornish migrants were miners or connected with mining was a misleading, if not dangerous myth. James Whetter, too, has always been at pains to impress upon me that farming has been as significant a part of the Cornish experience as mining. And A. L. Rowse, in commenting upon my works on the Cornish in Australia, has urged me consistently to "do the job properly" by considering the fortunes of those colonists involved in economic activities other than mining. Local and family historians have also asked me to "write-up" biographical sketches of the many Cornish pioneers about whom I have collected details. The pressure, then, to look at the Cornish role in the expansion of Adelaide and the South Australian agricultural frontier has been overwhelming.

Fortunately, the subject of South Australian expansion has already been examined in some depth by other writers—notably Michael Williams and D. W. Meinig—which made my attempts to set the experience of Cornish colonists against the background of this expansion so much easier than it might otherwise have been. Ron Gibbs' highly readable *A History of South Australia* was also most useful as a source of background material, as were the numerous other Cornish and Australian titles that I consulted in the course of my research.

Much of the material in this book is drawn from my doctoral thesis "The Cornish in South Australia", and so acknowledgement is due here to the many who helped with its compilation, most notably the University of Adelaide itself and my former tutor, John Playford. John Tregenza talked to me about his own research in the field, Ian Auhl provided numerous insights into the Central Hill Country and afforded all kinds of practical support, Jim Faull acquainted me with research undertaken by College of Advanced Education students into the question of Cornish social and economic mobility in the colony, the late May Cocks introduced me to the Cornish Association of South Australia, and Roslyn Paterson—herself a descendent of one of the area's first Cornish settlers—introduced me to the farming communities of northern Yorke Peninsula and shared with me her infectious enthusiasm for the region's past.

Most importantly, my wife Jane accompanied me on all my "jaunts" (as she would say) into the depths of rural South Australia—in the height of summer and the heart of winter—and assisted me in various areas of research, especially with her meticulous analysis of the Shipping Passenger Lists.

The Barr Smith Library, the State Library of South Australia (in particular its Archives, Newspaper, Reference and South Australian sections), the Parkin-Wesley Library, the Royal Institution of Cornwall (in particular its curator, H. L. Douch) and Cornwall County Record Office were all most helpful and gave permission for illustrations from their respective collections to be reproduced here. The National Library of Scotland has been especially co-operative, turning-up copies of rare South Australian publications and arranging for the copying of important illustrations.

My friend Elizabeth Yeardley went to great lengths to find the appropriate version of "We're Bound For South Australia", and took enormous pains in the compilation of the maps which grace this book. Len Truran gave the final seal of approval to the book by undertaking its publication.

PHILIP PAYTON,
St Cleer, Cornwall
*March 1987*

# We're Bound for South Australia

For South Australia I am bound,
Heave away! Haul away!
South Australia will be me home,
And we're bound for South Australia!
Heave away! Haul away!
Heave away you Ruler King,
And we're bound for South Australia

My wife is standin' on the quay,
Heave away! Haul away!
The tears do start as she waves to me,
And we're bound for South Australia!
Heave away! Haul away!
Heave away you Ruler King,
And we're bound for South Australia

Oh, fare-ye-well, now fare ye-well
Heave away! Haul away!
Oh, fare-ye-well, now fare-ye well,
And we're bound for South Australia!
Heave away! Haul away!
Heave away you Ruler King,
And we're bound for South Australia

Anon, nineteenth-century

# Introduction

In recent years the examination of the nineteenth-century mass emigration from Cornwall has become a clearly defined field of Cornish studies. Perhaps predictably, the main emphasis has been on the migration of Cornish miners and the nature of the mining commuities that they established overseas. Certainly, A. C. Todd and John Rowe have dealt almost exclusively with the miners, while A. L. Rowse's *The Cornish in America*, wide-ranging though it is, tends to emphasise the impact and influence of the *Cornish miners* in the USA. In a sense, this preoccupation with the miners is both inevitable and desirable. Numerically, they were probably the major occupational group amongst the male emigrants (though they probably did not constitute an overall majority) and, once overseas, they made an impact that was recognisably "Cornish". Not only did they help to build new mining industries based on Cornish practice, but also they created—for economic and geographical reasons—Cornish com-munities with distinctive Cornish social and cultural patterns. Non-mining Cornish migrants who did not settle in the mining towns were less likely to remain so overtly "Cornish" or to make an impact that could be defined so specifically as Cornish.

But, that said, it remains the case that a vast proportion of the nineteenth-century Cornish emigrants—many of the males and almost all of the females (only rarely does one read of Cornish bal-maidens working in overseas mines)—were not miners and, in Cornwall or in their new homes abroad, were employed in industries unconnected with mining. Their lives and progress are just as much a part of the Cornish emigrant experience, and they are therefore worthy of greater historical treatment than they have received hitherto. And, contrary to initial expectations, their "Cornishness" was not always lost in the colonial melting-pot, the background in Cornwall often affecting their economic, social or political activities overseas.

This rather brief effort looks at the fortunes of those who were not miners (or, alternatively, those miners who sought other occupations when once abroad) in one specific, but in several ways perhaps typical, area—the colony of South Australia. The theme is a simple one, to investigate the role of the Cornish in the opening-up of South Australia, in particular the expansion of its agricultural frontier. Necessarily, the approach is often anecdotal rather than analytical, for we must never forget that the "materials" with which we deal were once real people and not mere statistics—a fact that should be reflected in the narrative. Most of them were brave and long-suffering souls, folk who had seen much hardship in Cornwall, who had endured sometimes appalling sea-journeys to reach their new homes, and who—once in South Australia—were confronted not with a "promised land" but instead an up-hill battle against heat, drought, sandy-blight and mallee scrub. In many ways it is the ordinary people who are the heroes of Australian history and, at the risk of sounding a little arrogant, one sometimes reflects that there is an almost mystical nature about this kind of research: the re-discovery of individuals whose contributions had been long-since forgotten, whose deaths had sunk them into an undeserved but no doubt inevitable obscurity.

In so many ways the story of the expansion of the South Australian frontier is reminiscent of the experience in the other Australasian colonies, or indeed of the frontier expansion in North America. But, as Derek Whitelock and others have noted, South Australia's history has (rather like Cornwall's) always been one of "difference". South Australia was, from the very beginning in 1836, a "Paradise of Dissent" in which religious nonconformity flourished and social mobility was encouraged. It was also a "free" colony, unlike the surrounding Penal settlements, and it was the first Australian colony to establish a metaliferous mining industry. Moreover, throughout the nineteenth-century there was a continual enthusiasm for expansion, a conscious enthusiasm born originally of the drive, energy, and fervent idealism of the colony's founding fathers. And the immigrants, of course, Cornish amongst them, were also fired by this enthusiasm and became part of the expansionist process.

Part of this expansion, as intimated above and as made clear in the writer's *The Cornish Miner in Australia*, was the development of the mining industry. It may well be true, as P. R. Dunlop has argued, that it is the Cornish miners who ought to be honoured as the pioneers of South Australian development in the colonial era. But, at the same time, it is equally true that the actual process of "winning the land"—clearing the bush, establishing farms, laying-out townships—was the real stuff of colonisation, a role performed primarily by the agriculturalists who settled the land and the artizans who followed in their wake. Thus, just as a great many Cornish emigrants to South Australia were not miners, so South Australian expansion was in part dependent upon economic activity other than mining.

It would, of course, be naive to suggest that there was an absolute distinction between the miners and "the rest", or that there were no connections between the growth of mining and other forms of expansion. The miner-turned-farmer became a familiar figure in South Australia in the second half of the last century, many of the Cornish miners having had some experience as part-time agriculturalists on smallholdings at home. Indeed, the miner's ability to win a living from the colony's virgin land, in often difficult conditions, no doubt derived in part from the situation in Cornwall, described in 1831 by J. Britton and E. W. Brayley, where,

> Some of the landowners have . . . very judiciously leased out the better parts (of waste land) in lots of about three acres to labouring miners for ninety-nine years, determinable on three lives, on condition that each occupant builds a cottage and cultivates the soil. For this plot the tenant is required to pay an annual rent of ten shillings. This practice has tended to improve the appearance of the county, whilst the industrious miner is materially benefitted in health, in moral habits, and in property . . . .

Further, it is clear that there was an important link between mining development and the process of "winning the land", for not only did townships spring up in response to the opening of mines, but also the growth of mining generated other forms of economic activity. The importance of revenue-earning copper exports and the multiplier effects of wages paid to mine employees are obvious considerations, but of at least equal significance was the impetus to *agricultural* expansion provided by mining development. Michael Williams, in his *The Making of the South Australian Landscape*, showed that "The mines at Burra and Kapunda focussed attention on the Central Hill Country", while W. S. Kelly noted in his *Rural Development in South Australia* that increased demand caused by the Victorian

Gold Rush led to ". . . a remarkable concentration upon wheat-growing in open country on the Adelaide Plains . . .". Similarly, Charles Fenner argued in *South Australia: A Geographical Study* that the potential of Yorke Peninsula as an agricultural area was ". . . brought into prominence by the discoveries of copper in the north of this region". In his masterly study, *On the Margins of the Good Earth*, D. W. Meinig adds that even "Farther north mining had a noticeable though much smaller influence upon the settlement pattern."

The story of Cornishmen in South Australia, therefore, is not one involving an absolute division between "the miners" and "the rest". This book, however, is concerned principally with the fortunes of those Cornish migrants in South Australia who were involved in economic activities other than mining. Mines and miners, then, will feature only when they shed some light upon the expansion of the South Australian agricultural frontier. For the rest, it is the "non-miners" who shall for once enjoy the limelight.

# CHAPTER 1

## Paradise of Dissent—A Model Colony

The expansion of the agricultural frontier is perhaps *the* great epic in the history of South Australia. It was the very stuff of colonisation, the physical act of wresting the wilderness from nature and imposing the mark of European civilisation and order upon it. It was also an inexorable process which, though having peaks and troughs (the 1830s, 1850s and 1870s were years of expansion, the early 1840s and 1880s those of stagnation), persisted throughout the last century. This expansion was, of course, the realisation and manifestation of the hopes and dreams of South Australia's immigrants. As such it was an expression of South Australia's own ethos, a fruition of the ideals of the early founding fathers who had fought, not only for the foundation of South Australia, but for the establishment there of a particular form of colonisation.

The colony of South Australia was founded relatively late in the history of the Antipodes, two centuries after the "discovery" of the continent by Dutch seamen and nearly fifty years after the arrival of the first white settlers in New South Wales in 1788. Convict depots had been established in Van Diemen's Land (later Tasmania) in 1803 and 1804, and later other convicts were settled at Moreton Bay in the north of New South Wales in what was to become the colony of Queensland. Although the colony of Victoria was not proclaimed until 1850, it had been settled well before that date as part of New South Wales. And even Swan River colony (later Western Australia) predated South Australia's foundation by seven years, having been created in 1829.

Exploration went hand-in-hand with colonisation, and, although South Australia was not settled until 1836, it was not entirely an unknown land before that date. Dutch sailors had sailed along the southern coast of Australia as early as 1627 (and they were little impressed by it), while the Frenchmen d'Entrecasteaux and Baudin and the Englishman James Grant had also visited South Australian shores. But two names stand out in the history of the early exploration of South Australia, those of Matthew Flinders and Charles Sturt. Flinders was an Officer in the Royal Navy and had served with Captain William Bligh, the controversial Cornishman who later became Governor of New South Wales. In 1801 Flinders was commissioned by the Admiralty to make a survey of the Australian coast-line, and he reached the southern coast of Australia in his ship the "Investigator" in January of 1802. He discovered Kangaroo Island, and was responsible for naming many of South Australia's coastal physical features—Spencer's Gulf, St. Vincent's Gulf, Cape Catastrophe, Port Lincoln, Mount Lofty, and a number of others. In so doing, he carefully plotted, for the first time, the coast of South Australia.

Flinders' great contribution to the future settlement of South Australia was that he was the first to make detailed information of any kind available about the south-central coast of the continent. Similarly, Charles Sturt's exploration was an impetus to colonisation in that he too was able to give first-hand and accurate accounts of the new districts he encountered. Sturt's principal interest was in the course of the great inland rivers of Australia, and in 1829 he set out on the Murrumbidgee, moving east to west, in New South Wales. He moved far enough along the Murrumbidgee to discover its confluence with the Murray, and he followed the course of this new river as it turned southwards into what would later be South Australian territory. Sturt travelled on to the mouth of the Murray at Lake Alexandrina, and he was impressed by the ever-improving nature of the countryside and its resources. Sturt published the accounts of his expeditions in a two-volume work in 1833, and his report on South Australia was highly favourable and gave encouragement to those seeking to establish a new colony in Australia. He wrote:

> . . . it would appear that a spot has, at length, been found upon the south coast of New Holland, to which the colonist might venture with every prospect of success, and in whose valleys the exile might hope to build for himself and his family a peaceful and prosperous home. All who have ever landed upon the eastern shore of St. Vincent's Gulf, agree as to the richness of its soil, and the abundance of its pasture.

There was certainly at least one group of men in the United Kingdom anxious to find just such a "spot" in which to begin a new settlement. These men were liberals—dissenters and others who wished to escape what they saw as a lack of civil and religious liberty in Britain, and utilitarians who had witnessed the failings and shortcomings of the other Australian colonies and desired to try a new scheme of "systematic colonisation".

In the early decades of the nineteenth century, Christian religions in the United Kingdom were only just becoming equal in and before the law. The Test and Corporation Acts, which had inhibited the taking of office by dissenters, were repealed in 1828, and Catholic Emancipation was secured in 1829. Nevertheless, in terms of social status, great inequalities remained and certain disabilities were not yet eradicated: dissenters were not permitted to marry in their own chapels, and their burial rites had to be conducted according to the English Book of Common Prayer.

In the same way, many felt that civil liberties in the United Kingdom were also only theoretical. They were, many argued, dependent upon birth, rank, and property; as indeed were opportunities for advancement in social and economic fields. Many, too, remembered the repression that had existed during and after the Napoleonic Wars. Even in the 1830s, on the eve of the foundation of South Australia, many could recall those dark days after 1815 which had witnessed Peterloo, the Derbyshire Insurrection, the Cato Street Conspiracy, and other manifestations of discontent and repression. Indeed, the disenchantment of the Post-Napoleonic era led to growing opposition to the existing order. Many began to argue that individuals should not hold social station, economic wealth, or political power by virtue of birth alone, and others opposed the patronage, nepotism, and sinecures that existed within Government departments.

Liberal attention was also turned to the question of Parliamentary Reform, but for many Radicals the "Great Reform Act" of 1832 was a mere concession rather than a victory, while for others the Whigs—along with the whole atmosphere of the "Reforming Thirties"—were far too cautious. Electoral malpractice, of course, survived the attack of 1832. It was many years before the political influence of local landowners was diminished, and the secret ballot was not achieved until 1872. Chartism was

3

indicative of the continuing discontent, as was the agitation surrounding the Anti-Corn Law League. But a number lost faith in the possibility of further reform at home and decided instead to try to build a reformed society overseas, to reflect their ideals in the social, religious, political and economic order of a new land. Thus, as Douglas Pike has written, "South Australia was settled in 1836 by men whose professed ideals were civil liberty, social opportunity, and equality for all religions."

This, more than anything, accounted for the colony's developing sense of "difference", but it was also symptomatic of a changing attitude to colonisation in the United Kingdom. It should be remembered that in the early decades of the nineteenth-century there were few notions of imperialistic expansion, and Empire "jingoism" did not emerge as a significant force until after the passing of the era of Mid-Victorian prosperity when the threat to Britain's pre-eminent position from other powers became apparent. Instead, early colonisation was justified on the grounds of developing trade (or for strategic reasons to protect existing trade), and the actual movement of emigrants from the "mother country" to the colonies was advocated on the Malthusian principle of removing surplus population. The transportation of convicts to New South Wales and Van Diemen's Land may have been one application of this principle, as was certainly the "pauper emigration" to Upper Canada. Transportation and pauper emigration, however, came in for strong criticism from utilitarian liberals whose general objection to the practices was articulated in a leading article in *The Times*, which declared

> We have no right to cast out among other nations, or on naked shores, either our crime or our poverty. This is not the way in which a great and wealthy people, a mother of nations, ought to colonize.

Foremost amongst the utilitarians of this persuasion was Edward Gibbon Wakefield, a man whom historians have argued is, above all others, to be honoured as founder of South Australia. Certainly, he was a colonisation theorist of considerable importance. Instead of convicts and paupers, Wakefield wanted to see the new colonies peopled with enterprising

4

businessmen, good yeoman farmers, and honest labourers anxious to improve their lot. His ideas appeared in a series of articles and other publications between 1830 and 1833, and in 1830 he and his colleague Robert Gouger founded their "National Colonisation Society".

Wakefield, at that time, was not thinking specifically of South Australia, but was addressing his schemes to British territories in general. His Society and its ideas created considerable interest, and eminent liberal thinkers such as Jeremy Bentham and John Stuart Mill became associated with its activities. Indeed, Bentham was to write in support of Wakefield's plans for future colonisation in Australia, (although it must be admitted that his views do seem still a trifle Malthusian and not quite those of Wakefield). He wrote that renewed colonisation in Australia, on a systematic principle, would relieve

. . . a great part of the remaining portion of the Mother Country from the pressure of a continually increasing state of indigence from which they cannot at present be relieved but by a continually increasing tax imposed upon the people of all degrees above the lowest in the scale of opulence.

It would also afford,

. . . a security against all future increase of the existing pressure—a security which will not terminate till the Australian Continent contains a population as dense as the European.

Wakefield, as a utilitarian, believed in the "greatest happiness for the greatest number'. He felt that this end would be achieved, not through the redistribution of existing wealth, but rather by harnessing hitherto latent resources of land, labour and capital to create new wealth. And this was precisely what Wakefield's scheme of "systematic colonisation" was designed to achieve. Briefly, the broad structure of the plan was this: Land in the colony (or colonies) was to be sold at a fixed minimum price or above, and land sales were to be strictly regulated to prevent disorganisation similar to that which had occurred in New South Wales and Swan River Colony. Proceeds from the land sales would then be used primarily to assist the passage of bone fide immigrants. These colonists would be carefully selected to

5

ensure they were respectable, of good character, energetic, and also to create the right balance of ages and sexes. The volume and pace of immigration would be related closely to the amount of land being made available, and the settlement itself would expand in contiguous blocks to prevent the over-dispersion of the colonists (another failing at Swan River). Finally, there would be a considerable degree of local self-government, although, true to the liberal tradition, government intervention would be slight so as not to upset the harmonious interplay of economic forces or inhibit individual freedoms.

This optimistic scheme, far happier than that of "pauper emigration", engendered amongst many in the United Kingdom a new attitude to colonisation; and the prospects of emigration began to appeal, not only to the "down-and-outs" ready to grasp at any utopian solution, but to middle-class and working people eager for an opportunity to "get on" in life. After numerous set-backs, Wakefield managed finally to have a Bill presented before Parliament to secure a charter to colonise South Australia on the systematic principle. It was passed finally in both Houses, and received Royal Assent on 15 August 1834. This "Foundation Act" was a singular document in several respects—one being the legal fiction that South Australia was not a colony as such but rather a Province of the United Kingdom, a feature of South Australia's already developing sense of "difference". The Act handed most of the responsibility for the colonisation process to a Board of Commissioners, thus giving the colony a curious "double government" until 1857, involving both the Commissioners and the British Government, and enhancing still further South Australia's unorthodox constitutional identity. The colony's first Governor was Captain John Hindmarsh, another Naval Officer, and he arrived in South Australia in the wake of the first colonists at the end of 1836. The official Proclamation of the colony was read by Hindmarsh at Glenelg, a few miles from the site selected to become the City of Adelaide, on the afternoon of December 28 1836.

Although the practical difficulties of settlement combined with a severe financial crisis in the early 1840s to force a partial abandonment of "systematic colonisation", the Wakefieldian heritage remained of vital importance to South Australia and its separate identity. As late as 1890, it was still hailed as "A Model Colony" by Henry Cornish in his book *Under the Southern Cross*, and its utilitarian and nonconformist flavour (to which the Cornish contributed in no small measure) earned it a second and equally apt description—that of "Paradise of Dissent". In terms of actual numbers, the nonconformists were never an overwhelmingly dominant group in the colony—even in the earliest days—but their relative strength, influence and importance was far greater than that of the dissenters in the United Kingdom or in any other British possession. And, moreover, those Anglicans who settled in the colony were generally middle-class people—anxious for socio-economic improvement—whose aspirations and political views were largely in tune with those of the nonconformists. South Australia at its foundation, then, not only had its own recognisable and individual identity (as had Cornwall), but also it was developing a religious and social climate in which the Cornish, with their liberal and nonconformist leaning, could hardly fail to thrive.

In the late 1830s, while the handful of early colonists were struggling to establish their new homes, supporters of Wakefield and the South Australian adventure were mounting in the United Kingdom a propaganda campaign to impress upon the general public the particular advantages of the new colony and the systematic principle on which it had been founded. One such supporter was John Stephens, the son of a Cornish miner-turned-Methodist-minister, who came from an old Cornish family associated for centuries with the boroughs of Helston and Tregony. It is clear that Stephens' Cornish Methodist background was important in moulding his outlook, for in later years he was to play an important role in the defence of religious and civil liberty in the colony. However, his intimate involvement with South Australia began even before he had left the shores of Britain.

Stephens' publicity work on behalf of South Australia culminated in the publication, in London in 1839, of his book *The Land of Promise* in which he advocated emigration to the colony. He was a true adherent of Wakefield's system, as evidenced by his opening remarks in the first chapter of his book:

Land, capital, and labour, are the three grand elements of wealth,

7

and the art of colonization consists of transferring capital and labour from countries where they are in excessive proportion to the quantity of fertile land, to countries where there is plenty of fertile land, but neither capital nor labour.

To illustrate that South Australia was indeed a "fertile land" (for many had heard that it was an arid desert), Stephens went on to give encouraging descriptions of the Adelaide plain, and to dwell at some length on the beauties of the countryside near Cape Jervis, along the River Murray, and on Kangaroo Island. To give credence to his arguments, he quoted from enthusiastic letters sent home by the early settlers, and concluded that,

> All the authenticated accounts we have seen, agree to the fertility of the soil, and most settlers speak quite rapturously on the subject, comparing it to the richest parts of our own country.

And instead of drawing his readers' attentions to the extreme heat of the Antipodean summers, Stephens pointed out that in fact the South Australian climate was a cure for a great many ills, including asthma. For those who were still not convinced, he added the testimony of one colonist who wrote that ". . . in South Australia at least, the climate of Paradise appears to have survived the fall."

That Stephens' comments were addressed, not to paupers, but to respectable working men and to the middle-classes, is evident in the way in which he attempted to illustrate the superiority of South Australia over other colonies. He noted that South Australia did not experience the degradation and lawlessness of the Penal colonies—and that in fact the colony was entirely free of convict settlers—and he showed that the colony had been founded in an orderly and business-like fashion, unlike the disorganised settlements at Swan River and Port Phillip. South Australia had also, he said, none of the unpleasant conditions that were to be encountered in African and Asian colonies. And, moreover, he stressed that South Australia was, unlike Canada, free from the threat of Popery—an important consideration for many middle-class dissenters (Cornish among them). Indeed, he noted the conditions of religious liberty that had been established in the colony, and was at pains to point out that the Wesleyan, Baptist, and Independent denominations were already thriving in

8

South Australia. His conclusion was that,

> The superiority of South Australia, not only over the British colonies in North America, and Africa, and Asia, but also over New South Wales, Swan River, King George's Sound, and Van Diemen's Land, themselves, appear to be established on testimony that cannot be disputed. Persons who have had experience of all the other colonies in question agree in awarding the palm of decided excellence to the new settlement.

In liberal, dissenting Cornwall—on the eve of the "Hungry Forties"—all this sounded too good to be true, and local migration agents lost no time in seeking out suitable emigrants for the new colony of South Australia.

# CHAPTER 2

## *"And We're Bound For South Australia"*

The extensive migration from Cornwall to South Australia in the nineteenth-century has been analysed in some depth in the author's *The Cornish Miner in Australia*, but inevitably that analysis was presented with the particular case of the miners very much in view. Fortunately, there is also considerable (and hitherto unpublished) material which sheds light upon the parallel emigration of Cornish agriculturalists and artizans—who were at least as hard hit as the miners by the disasterous 1840s, and perhaps more so in the agricultural depression of the 1870s. Some of the earliest Cornish emigrants, indeed, were inhabitants of the largely non-mining district of North Cornwall, the *West Briton* noting in April 1832 that

> The rage for emigration that now prevails in the north of this county is wholly unprecedented in Cornwall; in different parishes from 200 to 300 persons each, have either departed or are preparing to leave . . . .

This "rage" continued throughout the 1830s, which were years of discontent and agitation for reform, and the foundation of South Australia in 1836 provided an important new destination for potential emigrants from Cornwall. Cornwall was identified almost immediately as a likely source of suitable colonists, and was visited by John Marshall, one of the South Australian migration agents from London. He was followed by Rowland Hill, then Secretary of the South Australian Commissioners, and local agents were appointed to act in the various parts of Cornwall. Their persuasive approach echoed that of John Stephens in his *The Land of Promise*, one of the Cornish agents, Isaac Latimer, declaring in his poster "Free Emigration to Port Adelaide" that South Australia was

> . . . well-watered—and there have never been any complaints from the colonists of a want of this valuable element; on the contrary, the letters from Cornishmen who have written home are very satisfactory on this point. It should be borne in mind that

complaints of a scarcity of water do not relate to Port Adelaide, but to other settlements not connected with South Australia.

As their posters and newspaper advertisements indicated, the local migration agents—true to the principles of systematic colonisation—were interested in all working men and women in gainful employment (and *not* paupers) who were sober, industrious, and of good character. In one poster issued on 27 February 1839 Latimer cited twenty-one desired occupations, but in practice anyone with a trade would be given an opportunity to apply for free passage. At the same time, the agents were interested specifically in receiving applications from married couples (or alternatively single men to be accompanied by their single sisters) under the age of thirty. But again, there does seem to have been some relaxation of the rules on occasions, as agents would sometimes encourage couples well over the age limit to submit applications for free passage.

Fortunately, the applications for free passage to South Australia for the period 1836 to 1840 have survived. 941 of these applications were lodged in Cornwall, ten per cent of all applications lodged in Britain and Ireland, a figure which—given the relatively small population and geographic size of Cornwall—makes interesting comparison with the five percent for Devon and Somerset combined and the thirty-five for London and the adjoining Home Counties. Cornwall, then, had already become a significant source of South Australian colonists, with over 500 of these applications, corresponding to some 1400 persons, actually being accepted. Appendix 3 shows a detailed breakdown of all Cornish these applications, analysed according to sex, year of application, occupation and parish.

Even in 1836, at the dawn of migration to South Australia and months before Governor Hindmarsh made his historic proclamation at Glenelg, applications for free passage had been received from five Cornish families. Down in the far west of Cornwall, at St Levan in the Penwith peninsula, James Bennetts—a thirty year old carpenter and wheelwright—and his thirty-four year old wife carefully submitted their application, dated 21 April 1836, pointing out that they were keen to purchase land in the new colony. Bennetts' kinsman, Pascoe Grenfell, a joiner and wheelwright from nearby Madron, was also anxious to emigrate.

He had a thirty year old wife, three sons (aged 10, 3 and 1) and three daughters (aged 11, 8 and 6). But he himself was thirty-four years old, four years over the formal age limit. Worried that his age might prove a disability, he stressed that in the last resort he would be prepared to pay his own way.

Still in the Penwith peninsula, was John Richards, described as an agricultural labourer and sheepshearer from Sancreed parish, and further east—at Falmouth—there was a similar application from another John Richards, a labourer. In 1836 the interest of the population in the more easterly parts of Cornwall does not seem to have been aroused, although one application was submitted by James Harme, a farm labourer from Warleggan—a rural parish on the southern slopes of Bodmin Moor. It is clear, however, that James' application was either rejected or withdrawn, for he is again found applying for free passage to South Australia three years later in 1839.

By 1837 this trickle of applicants had turned to a veritable flood, some 79 being received during the year from adult males (often in their capacity as heads of large households), with another 23 from single and widowed women (married women were included on their husband's applications and were not recorded separately). Again, the greatest interest in South Australia was exhibited in the more heavily populated, western parts of Cornwall, with Gwennap and Penryn heading the list and Falmouth running a close third.

We have a fascinating insight into one knot of emigrants among these 1837 applicants from Falmouth and Penryn (who set sail in the ship "Trusty") in the correspondence of Marmaduke Laurimer and Samuel Robins. Some months after his arrival in South Australia, Laurimer wrote home to Falmouth, his lengthy epistle later forming part of an emigration poster issued in that district by the local agent, A. B. Duckham. The account he gave is invaluable, for it is an eye-witness' report by one of the early colonists of the very first attempts to transform the wilderness:

> I should have written before, but it takes some time for a person to be in a new colony to know its ins and outs. In the first place, no farming has yet been done in the colony; not an acre of corn planted; nothing but a few sections of 80 acres each, has been

ditched; the colonists were not in possession of their country lands before last May; they have lived on their means the while . . . (but) . . . Adelaide . . . which only two months ago was a desert, is rising rapidly, . . . Work, I expect, will be very brisk near winter; the ground then, is soft: plenty of heavy rains fall in the winter, and there is neither frost nor snow . . . it is a fine climate, and very healthy. South Australia is one of the most beautiful countries in the world; all the splendid descriptions of it at home were strictly true: its fine rich plains without a tree upon them; its trees are evergreens, its mountains forming a boundary at the eastern direction of the town; its soil rich as nature can make it . . . .

Laurimer was anxious that other Cornishmen should learn about South Australia, asking his mother ". . . to inform Dr Simmons of Flushing what I have said of the colony". But his letter was also full of news concerning those friends from Cornwall who had accompanied him in the "Trusty". He wrote,

Alice Champion is married, a very good match she has got, her husband was in the Van Diemen's Land Company's Service . . . . The Montgomerys are doing well, Robert will be a father before you receive this letter . . . I have seen Mallett, Robins, and Organ, the latter lost his son at sea—they are all doing well. If Mrs Mallett could see her younger son, she would kiss him to death. He has grown such a nice little fellow.

Alice Champion was a member of the Champion family of Penryn and Mylor, and the Montgomery family mentioned by Laurimer also hailed from Mylor. On the date of his application (23 December 1837), Robert Montgomery—described as a kitchen gardener and agricultural labourer—was 27 years old, his wife a mere 19. Then they had no children although, as Laurimer intimated, one was born soon after their arrival on South Australian soil. Early in 1838 two other members of the family, 18 year old Sampson, a husbandman, and 16 year old Mary, a mantua maker, submitted applications to join Robert in the colony.

The Mallett family, from Penryn, consisted of 20 year old Henry, a "butcher, shepherd and farmer", his 25 year old wife, and his daughters aged three and one. There was also 15 year old John, another butcher, almost certainly Henry's younger brother. The Organs, again from Penryn, comprised 25 year old

Benjamin—a saddle and harness maker in Market Street—together with his wife, aged 22, and their child aged 16 months. Samuel Robins, a mason from Penryn, was another of the "Trusty" emigrants and, like Marmaduke Laurimer, has achieved a certain immortality through the survival of one of his letters sent home to Cornwall. When he left Penryn, Robins had promised his sister that he would return to Cornwall after ten years (a common enough aspiration, many Cornish emigrants hoping to earn enough abroad to enable them to return home relatively wealthy), but by 1846 that prospect had ceased to be attractive. In October of that year he wrote to his sister:

> You remind me of my promise to return home in ten years; I was young and foolish when I uttered that speech, and I hope you will not expect me to leave a country like this . . . I cannot help thinking how inconsistent you write; you give me a wretched account of things at home, and expect me to leave a country which is flourishing fast . . . . It is a pity you make remarks about this country, when you know nothing of it. A handsome expression to tell me I am bringing up my children unnamed savages . . . I am determined to stop were (sic) I am and nothing you can say will alter my mind.

Despite the particular enthusiasm for South Australia displayed by the Falmouth-Penryn district, each month of 1837 saw information regarding the new colony finding its way into ever more remote corners of Cornwall, so that applications were received from families and individuals in some of the more obscure and outlying parishes—from Stithians in the west to Lewannick in the east. In 1837 26 male applicants were described as "labourers", the major occupational group, and they came from all over Cornwall—Richard Cornelius from Redruth Highway, Zacharias Gray from Holmbush, St Austell, William Hoskyn from Penquite, St Breward, Thomas Sleep from Linkinhorne . . . . Others had more specific or skilled trades; there were, for example, eight carpenters, seven masons, six shoemakers and six (only) miners. Again, there was a fair geographic spread amongst these more skilled applicants—William Carne was a carpenter and joiner from Helston Road, Penryn, J. Paul was a boot and shoemaker from Bodinnick-by-Fowey, and William Scown was a mason and bricklayer from

Launceston. William Cocking, another of the Falmouth applicants, was a 47 year old mason who, despite his age, was able to impress the agents by stressing that he had had 19 years experience in the Corps of Sappers and Miners and had acquired, perhaps, pioneering skills which would be of particular value in the infant colony. In the end, most of these 1837 applicants were accepted as migrants, those not sailing in the "Trusty" travelling in the "Emma", "Red Admiral" and "Katherine S. Forbes".

In 1838 the number of Cornish applicants expanded to reach 170, from areas as far-flung as Torpoint, St Blazey, St Ewe, Wendron and Altarnun. Gwennap was the major source of applicants (some 24 all told) but, although the centre of the copper-mining world, none of those expressing interest was a miner. Instead, there were men like Richard Bowden, a stonecutter, Samuel Bray, a gardener from Trevethan, and Robert Corner, a cordwainer. Elsewhere in Cornwall the story was the same, there being only two miner-applicants amidst many variously described as farmers, husbandmen and agricultural labourers, together with an impressive range of skilled tradesmen: there was a blacksmith from St Dominick, a harnessmaker from Calstock, a painter and glazier from Hayle.

By 1839 the total applications had more than doubled, reaching 360. But although 45 applicants were miners, the vast majority were of course engaged in other occupations. The miners were not yet the dominant group, for there were 57 agricultural labourers, together with considerable numbers of farmers, carpenters and masons. Similarly, several of the "new" areas from which applications were appearing for the first time— such as St Goran and Gerrans on the Roseland Peninsula and Landrake and North Petherwin in East Cornwall—were agricultural rather than mining districts. Again, many of these 1839 applicants were accepted, voyaging to South Australia in the "Somersetshire", "Cleveland", "Recovery", and the ill-fated "Java" in which a number of passengers died during a long and disease-ridden journey to Port Aelaide.

In 1840 there was a slight slackening of interest in the colony, the number of applications dropping to just over 300, although in the Camborne-Redruth and adjoining copper mining districts the trend was the reverse—the number of miner-applicants rising sharply to 132. Even so, the majority of applicants continued to be non-miners, their range of occupations and geographic origins continuing to be as wide as ever. There was 40 year old Thomas Bonython, for example, a shoemaker from St Columb Minor, John Bossnall, a tailor from St Thomas (near Launceston), and Thomas Smith, a net and ropemaker from St Clements (near Truro). Amongst the ladies were Mary Tregea, a domestic servant from Perranporth, Mary Ann Arnall, a dressmaker from Camelford, and Jane Dunstan, a farm servant from Veryan.

The wide range of skilled occupations represented in the applications for free passage indicates that the migration agents were successful in recruiting the right kind of people for the colony. Tradesmen and yeomen, artizans and good, honest workers were those sought for South Australia, whilst those in debt or on parish relief were to be avoided. However, whilst the agents were not interested in abject paupers, poverty in nineteenth-century Cornwall was a relative thing. A great many of the "honest labourers", and even the skilled tradesmen, lived in conditions that were appalling by any standards, and all were affected by economic downturns. Indeed, economic factors—the desire to escape poverty at home, and the hope of a life of "plenty" overseas—were the strongest and most consistent motivations for migration from Cornwall to South Australia in the nineteenth-century. This can be seen at the "macro" level where the nature and volume of emigration was linked clearly to economic fluctuations, but it can also be demonstrated, perhaps more poignantly, at the "micro" level where individual cases of hardship and suffering can be examined.

Typical of the plight of many in Cornwall was that of Samuel Stanton, born in St Cleer in 1829, who was placed in parish bondage as a child on the death of his parents. After some years of that institutionalised poverty he ran away, making his way eventually to New South Wales, and from there to South Australia. A contemporary account of Stanton's childhood experiences spoke of the ". . . frequent cruelties and comparative starvation . . ." he suffered while bound a parish apprentice, a state of affairs by no means atypical of that era.

The position of some was less extreme, but nevertheless still

16

parlous enough to make emigration very desirable, if not essential. Stephen Hicks, for example, was a penniless farmer from the North Cornish parish of St Mabyn who chose emigration as a potential solution to his problems after having read a favourable account of South Australia in the *Chambers Journal*—a popular magazine of the time which had embraced the cause of emigration. Similarly, Richard Best, the son of an impoverished labourer, was persuaded to secure a passage to the colony by Parson Childs, the then Vicar of St. Dennis. Best's father had struggled for years to keep his seven children, earning just one shilling per day, while Richard himself was sent out to work at the age of seven—as a cowhand—for only twopence a day. Such "deserving cases" could hardly fail to recommend themselves to the more humanitarian of the local literati, the village squires and vicars, who would often advise emigration as a means of easing poverty at home. Parson Childs, in particular, took a strong interest in the cause of emigration, often travelling the 40 miles or so from St Dennis to Plymouth to address the migrants on the eve of their departure from Britain.

Superimposed upon the fundamental economic motivations for emigration were often intensely personal considerations so that, whilst one may generalise, it is nevertheless instructive to examine individual situations. James Harvey and his sister Harriet, for example, left Cornwall for Port Adelaide in the "Buffalo" in 1836 to escape a family quarrel, their fare paid for them by their father as their presence in the family home was resented by their new stepmother. The emigration of George Venning, from Trebray in the parish of Altarnun, was prompted by quite different but equally personal considerations. George and his wife Grace (from neighbouring Trelin) had settled down to a mildly prosperous life as farmers, but George fell ill and was at length advised by his doctors to abandon the damp and misty wastes of Bodmin Moor and seek instead the drier climes of South Australia—where his failing health might have an opportunity to improve. Wisely, George listened to this advice, later becoming a successful farmer at Mount Barker Springs and Nairne in the Adelaide Hills.

Many experienced the Cornish wander-lust, as was the case of Thomas Champion—another of the Champions of

Mylor and Penryn—who had served in the Royal Navy for a time after the Napoleonic Wars but who later, tiring of the quieter life ashore, decided to seek his fortune anew in South Australia. This was not altogether an uncommon sentiment in sea-faring Cornwall, and certainly many looked on with envy as the graceful and majestic tall ships set sail from Cornish ports for colonies overseas. Philip Santo, a carpenter from Saltash who emigrated to South Australia in 1840, where he later became a prominent colonist and politician, recalled how people living in the Tamarside towns of Saltash and Torpoint were thus affected: ". . . ships leaving for distant colonies induced others to go too. When they saw ships going to Adelaide or elsewhere, they were induced to enquire and emigrate".

After the initial enthusiasm for South Australia, at the end of 1840 a brake was applied to emigration to the colony—which was in the grip of a sudden and potentially damaging financial crisis. Fortunately, tough action by the colony's Governor stemmed the flow of capital and labour from South Australia, and by 1844 the infant colony was again strong enough to resume full-scale immigration. Of course, the cessation of immigration had always been anathema to true adherents of the Wakefield doctrine. In the years after January 1841 the sale of waste lands in South Australia had swollen the immigration fund to £32,000 and, despite the revival of immigration in 1844, it grew to £100,000 by May 1847, when the Government sanctioned its full expenditure.

By then, of course, South Australia's mineral bonanzas had already been struck—silver-lead at Glen Osmond (near Adelaide) in 1841, copper at Kapunda in 1843 and at distant Burra Burra in 1845. Thereafter, the extent and nature of Cornish emigration to South Australia was determined largely by the fortunes of the Cornish and South Australian mining economies (the classic "push" and "pull" forces of migration), a trend perpetuated by the discovery in 1859–61 of the extensive northern Yorke Peninsula copper deposits. However, as the shipping passenger lists and other sources indicate, the emigration of copper miners and their famiies to South Australia was accompanied by a continuing and important emigration of Cornish men and women who were not connected directly with the mining industry.

For example, although much Cornish emigration to South

18

Australia in the mid and late 1840s was occasioned by demand for labour at Kapunda and Burra Burra, there was a parallel emigration of agriculturalists and other "non-miners" who were just as anxious to escape the dreadful effects of the "Hungry Forties" and its potato blight which had all but destroyed the Cornish crop on several successive seasons. In March 1847 the *Register* newspaper, published in Adelaide, expressed the view that Cornish farmers and husbandmen would be drawn to South Australia for "The people of Cornwall were . . . fully aware of the success which had crowned the labours of our indefatigable agriculturalists and their horticultural brethren . . .".

Certainly, during 1849 there was a considerable movement to South Australia from the Penwith district, and in 1850 there was a similar movement from the Lizard peninsula—50 persons leaving the agricultural parish of Mawgan-in-Meneage for the colony. Indeed, in the period 1841–51 the population of the Meneage had dropped by five per cent, the widespread emigration constituting a great loss to the friends and relatives who remained, a subdued atmosphere often filling homes—and sometimes whole villages—as a result. John Boaden wrote that when the Orchards left Mawgan-in-Meneage for South Australia in 1849, the whole parish felt a sense of loss—". . . the emigration of the Orchard family seemed to give a melancholy tinge to everything . . ."—and not surprisingly so, the Boadens and Orchards being related by marriage, and there being Orchards at Carrabone, Garras and Trelowarren Mill, and Boadens at Burncoose, Tregadjack, Gweek, Mawgan Churchtown and Bojorrow. Emigration could have profound effects upon hitherto tight, inter-meshed and often introspective "extended family" relationships.

In the 1850s and 1860s mining continued to determine the ebb and flow of Cornish emigration to South Australia. Between 1848 and 1860 the occupations of some 2,117 adult male Cornish migrants were recorded, of whom 1,797—or 84.9 per cent—were miners; and between 1862 and 1867, 1,007 adult male Cornish migrants were recorded, of whom 366—or 36.3 per cent—were miners. A considerable number continued, however, to be Cornishmen unconnected with mining. (Appendix 4 provides a detailed analysis of the occupations of adult Cornish immigrants

19

into South Australia in the period 1848–67 for whom occupations are recorded in the shipping passenger list and is based upon an analysis of the passenger lists 1845–89 conducted by Jane Payton.)

A similar mix of occupations to that of the early era of immigration is seen in the passenger lists for 1848–67. There were the usual agricultural labourers, shoemakers, wheelwrights, masons, carpenters, female domestic servants, seamstresses, and so on, an indication that the colony continued to require the same kind of immigrant as envisaged originally by the founding fathers. The shipping passenger lists are fragmentary and incomplete, to say the least, and vary tremendously in quality and attention to detail. But on occasions they are very good, providing telling insights into the social and occupational make-up of a particular ship's passengers. In the "Prince Regent" in 1849, for example, there were 60 Cornish migrants from a total of 280 passengers. Eight of the Cornishmen were miners, and the rest were spread through the usual range of occupations— Charles Carbis and Thomas Trelour were farm labourers, Sally Uren was a domestic servant, and Benedict Quick was a carpenter. Edward Teague was a mason, as was Richard Taylor, and Loveday and Elizabeth Richards were both servants. Similarly, in the "Omega" in 1851, there were 131 Cornish amongst the total of 335 passengers, including such individuals as a carpenter named Edwin Trevena and a domestic servant called Susan Saunders. Almost ten years later the mix had hardly changed, the 56 Cornish out of the "Ramillies'" 287 migrants including farm labourers, such as John Marks and James Pillern, and female servants like Sophia Paynter and Elizabeth Kemp.

Cornish immigration into South Australia came to a head in the early-to-mid 1860s, when most ships arriving at Port Adelaide carried sizeable Cornish groups. The "Morning Star" in 1863 carried 430 passengers, of whom 78 were Cornish, and— amongst the usual mass of copper miners—were individuals such as Richard Philips, a blacksmith, John Hammer, a carpenter, and Jane Berryman, a servant. The "Mary Shepherd", another of the 1863 arrivals at Port Adelaide, carried 66 Cornish out of a total of 375, while in 1864 and 1865 the Cornish numbers grew even more impressive—72 out of 366 on the "Adamant", 211 out of 315 on the "Queen Bee", 207 out of 383 on the "Clara", 100 out of 295 on the "Coldstream", 131 out of 331 on the "Peeress", 161 out of 288 on the "Cornwallis", 214 out of 358 on the "Lady Milton", 187 out of 408 on the "Lincoln", 175 out of 296 on the "Maori", 242 out of 388 on the "Gosforth", and so on. In 1866 the numbers subsided somewhat, although occasional ships did arrive with large numbers of Cornish on board—such as the "Salamanca" with its 162 Cornish migrants (out of a total of 368) and the "Canterbury" with its 97 Cornish out of 437. Writing many years later in the *People's Weekly* newspaper in April 1927, one of the "Canterbury" passengers recalled that,

> There was a considerable number of Cornish on board . . . . The Stockers, a musical family . . . John Opie, his wife, son, and two daughters (Temperance and Prudence) . . . the late Fred Hancock . . . George Treais and Tom Worth, single men . . . .They were natives of St Dominick parish, overlooking the Tamar, in the Royal Duchy.

In the late 1860s and early 1870s emigration to South Australia declined, as a result of Government policy, but in 1872 the flood gates were again opened—with the effect that between 1872 and 1879 some 7.0 per cent of the 24,339 recorded immigrants were from Cornwall. A crisis in the tin mining industry at home ensured that there continued to be significant numbers of miners amongst the Cornish migrants. But the 1870s were also a time of agricultural depression in the United Kingdom, with the effect of competition from North American produce being compounded by a series of extremely bad harvests at home. There were epidemics of foot-and-mouth disease and swine fever, and falling wheat prices contributed further to agrarian poverty throughout Britain and Ireland. The United Kingdom alone, of all the major European States, with its commitment to Free Trade and the economic philosophy of laissez-faire, was reluctant to protect the agricultural industry. As a result, wages fell and there was consequently a steady migration of young agricultural labourers and their families to the colonies—especially to Canada and Australia.

A Royal Commission into the causes of agricultural depression found Cornwall less badly hit than other areas as a result of its changing agricultural patterns—less wheat was being grown, and instead there had been a movement to horticulture and stock farming. Nevertheless, the depression—coming on top of the tin crisis—had the effect of boosting emigration from Cornwall, a significant number of arrivals at Port Adelaide in the 1870s being agricultural labourers and their families. Many, indeed, were attracted by South Australia's policy of rural expansion—the 1870s witnessing a new enthusiasm for rolling back the colony's frontiers of settlement, a policy associated closely with South Australia's Cornish Premier, James Penn Boucaut.

Immigration into South Australia continued intermittently into the 1880s, but by then the colony was becoming less attractive as a result of its own industrial and agricultural depression. In several respects the expansion of the 1870s had overstretched itself, the "long drought" of the late 1880s and 1890s not only halting but actually turning back the march of the agricultural frontier. Assisted immigration ceased in 1886, and thereafter—as the nineteenth century, and with it the colonial era, drew to a close—only a handful of Cornish migrants continued to arrive in South Australia. By 1886, however, perhaps as many as 16,000 Cornish people had landed in the colony. By the turn of the century the number of people of Cornish birth or descent could have been as high as 30,000—approximately 9 per cent of the total population—an indication not only of the extent of the Cornish immigration, but also of the impact of the Cornish upon South Australian society.

# CHAPTER 3

## *Adelaide and Environs*

Official, Government-sponsored colonisation of South Australia did not commence until 1836, but there had been a scattering of white settlers in the coastal regions before that date—a handful of whalers and sealers, and the occasional escaped convict from the Penal colonies. One nineteenth-century literary effort referred in somewhat romantic vein to "The Pirates and Wreckers of Kangaroo Island", lawless convict gangs which allegedly lived on the island prior to 1836. It was an evocative title with obvious Cornish allusions but, while there were certainly Cornishmen amongst the early convicts in Australia, there is little evidence to suggest Cornish involvement in these piratical and wrecking gangs—if, indeed, they did exist. We do know that one of Kangaroo Island's early sealers was a fellow called Bryant (a common enough West Country, if not specifically Cornish, name) and John Williams, one of the escapees who sought refuge on the island, may—from the evidence of his surname—have been Cornish or Welsh. Nothing else, however, indicates a Cornish presence in South Australia before 1836.

Although the principal settlement was established on the mainland, in what was to become the city of Adelaide, the first official colonists landed on Kangaroo Island. The South Australian Company's ship, the "Duke of York", arrived in Nepean Bay, Kangaroo Island, on 27 July 1836. A second ship, the "Lady Mary Pelham", arrived three days later, and the "John Pirie" dropped anchor on 16 August. Significantly, the first adult colonist to set foot upon South Australian soil was Samuel Stephens, one of the remarkable Stephens brothers who played such an important role in moulding the character of early South Australia. Samuel was the younger brother of John Stephens, the South Australian propagandist who was to write *The Land of Promise* and later become editor of the Adelaide *Register*. A third brother was Edward Stephens, a leader in the nonconformists' struggle against the Adelaide Establishment in the 1840s when, as chairman of the "Society for the Preservation

23

of Religious Freedom", he successfully opposed State aid to religious denominations. All three brothers were influenced profoundly by their father—the Rev. John Stephens, a Cornish miner, Methodist minister, and one-time President of the British Wesleyan Conference—and we can see in their activities, therefore, the subtle but important imprint of Cornwall.

Samuel Stephens, however, turned out to be the least successful of the three brothers in the colony, and his career in South Australia was such that it was unlikely to endear his memory to other Cornishmen. For despite the influence of his father and close business association with George Fife Angas (a prominent dissenter and philanthropist, and a founder of South Australia) he was by nature headstrong, quarrelsome and self-important. He arrived in South Australia as Colonial Manager of the South Australian Company with orders to establish a settlement and permanent whaling station on Kangaroo Island at a site to be called Kingscote. Stephens, however, chose a poor site for the settlement and, according to Douglas Pike, ". . . proved excitable, irresponsible, too conceited to take advice . . . and too foolish when drunk to keep the respect of his subordinates".

The anchorage at Kingscote settlement was too shallow, so that ships had to stand almost a quarter of a mile out to sea, the soil was infertile, the water in the newly-dug well was brackish, and there was little suitable timber for the construction of buildings. Stephens quarrelled with his officers, some of whom he dismissed, and the colonists themselves quickly became disillusioned with the whole enterprise. As a result, they became unruly and intemperence was widespread. When Governor Hindmarsh arrived on the mainland in December 1836, he ordered an inquiry into the mismanagement on Kangaroo Island. Stephens, however, continued to squander his company's assets, and in November 1837 he was removed from his position. He then went to the mainland where he lived until 1840, when he was killed in a riding accident.

Happily, the experience on the mainland was far less traumatic than that on Kangaroo Island. Although there were numerous practical problems, exacerbated as always by personality clashes, greater care had been taken with the selection of the site for the

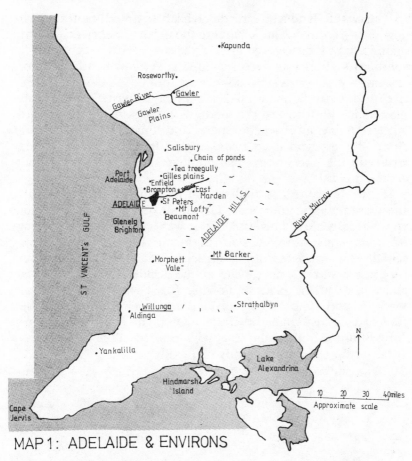

**MAP 1: ADELAIDE & ENVIRONS**

first mainland settlement. This was due largely to the pains of Colonel William Light, the colony's Surveyor General, who had examined possible sites at the Murray mouth, and on Yorke Peninsula and Eyre Peninsula, before rejecting them all in favour of Adelaide. He considered that the mouth of the Port Adelaide river, despite the surrounding swamplands (which soon led to it being dubbed "Port Misery"), would make a suitable deep water harbour. And Adelaide itself, he decided, ought to be situated some six miles inland on higher ground upon the coastal plain.

By January 1837 Light was busy planning Adelaide. He conducted a preliminary survey of 1042 acres in what was to be the city, the land thus made available straddling the River Torrens—North Adelaide lying to the north of the river, with the main bulk of the surveyed area to the south. At the centre of the southern section was Victoria Square, from which emanated a system of criss-crossing roads which formed Adelaide's distinctive grid pattern layout. Also distinctive were the extensive parklands "built in" to this pattern. Interestingly, one of those engaged to lay out Adelaide's parks and squares was W. Pengilly, from St Ives, who liked to boast that he had planted 100,000 trees during his term of employment with the colonial Government.

With the city thus established, Light turned his attention to the surrounding countryside. His survey of the country sections was painfully slow, however, for he was hampered by a shortage of equipment and trained staff. Light's health was also beginning to fail, and with mounting criticism of his lack of apparent progress with the country survey, he decided to resign. Shortly after, in 1839, he died. Following Light's resignation, survey work ground almost to a halt, and was not resumed until new staff had arrived from the United Kingdom—one of whom was John Phillips, from Camborne, who in Cornwall had worked as a surveyor for the Bassett family of Tehidy.

1. The very first dwellings at the proposed site for the City of Adelaide, sketched by William Light. From William Harcus, *South Australia*, 1876.

By 1838, then, a permanent and defined community was beginning to emerge. Adelaide was still, however, a collection of huts and simple timber buildings, at that stage little more than a large village perched on a small patch of cleared land adjacent to a vast and unknown wilderness. The early colonists had hoped to create in South Australia a "Britain in the Antipodes" but it was clear that in this unique and rather awesome environment something rather different would emerge. Inevitably, the first colonists were not beginning with an entirely clean slate upon which to write their ideas. South Australia was already settled by an Aboriginal people, and the European immigrants were severely constrained by the geographic and climatic conditions that they encountered. Heat, water-shortages, and inverted seasons were un-British in the extreme (there was never a chance of a "White Christmas" in Adelaide), and the countryside could never look like that of Britain. The eucalyptus tree, in its infinite forms, dominated the landscape, and the wild-life was decidedly unusual—kangaroos, wombats and goannas must have presented a strange spectacle to the newly-arrived immigrant unversed in the peculiarities of Antipodean fauna.

The impact of this singular environment was, of course, as profound for the Cornish as it was for other groups of colonists. An even cursory glance at their initial reactions to this strange and alien land reveals the enormity of the impact upon them. In 1911 Richard Best, from St Dennis, could still recall his first impressions of South Australia and how he felt upon his arrival in the new country:

> What are our thoughts! Well are they graven on my mind! For three months (at sea) our food had been assured without anxiety and little effort on our part. Where would tomorrow's meal come from? What welcome awaited us in this strange land! Had we made a mistake? Should we find ourselves stranded with the struggle of the Old Land renewed or would it be a stronger struggle in a new land commenced! How conflicting the thoughts and emotions that swayed us.

Some, like John Martin from Stithians, admitted that at first ". . . you would think that the land was good for nothing . ." but that growing familiarity with the colony would improve one's estimation of its worth. Charles Dunn, in a letter to a friend at

27

Hext Mill, Lewannick, noted that an immigrant's first impression depended largely on whether one arrived in summer or winter. He had landed at Port Adelaide during the summer months and ". . . gave a bad account of the country; it was then looking dry . . .". The winter rains, however, turned the vegetation green and luxuriant and he was persuaded to change his mind.

Thomas Sleep, from Falmouth, was unfortunate in that his father died soon after their arrival in Adelaide. Like many other colonists, Thomas was forced to spend his first weeks in the colony living in a tent—with his brother Samuel, his mother, and a young girl called Ann Pierce. He was determined, however, to make the best of things in South Australia, writing stoicly that "You can scarcely conceive how comfortable these tents are made". Others were indeed stimulated by the challenges of the new environment, it being said of Nicholas Dunstan from Constantine that he ". . . was so favourably impressed with the colony that he would not have cared had he been landed there quite unprepared". Similarly, William, Joseph and James Pedler wrote to their brother Thomas in Truro, noting that ". . . the only thing that makes us uncomfortable is the absence of our families".

Newly arrived settlers were always intrigued by the Aboriginal population, and in early South Australia the relationship betwen the whites and the natives was generally peaceful. The colonists' reactions, therefore, tended to be of wonder rather than fear, many describing—in letters written home—their first contacts with the local Kaurna tribe. Joseph Pedler, in a letter to one of his brothers at Perranarworthal, wrote that "The natives of the place are very civil . . .", while John Holman informed his father in South Petherwin that "The natives are quite harmless . . .". Thomas Davey, another Cornish immigrant, admitted that "We were very much surprised to see the natives . . ." but went on to echo the general opinion that the Aborigines were friendly and did not pose a threat to the new colony.

During 1838 the infant colony experienced a significant change of direction, when Hindmarsh was replaced as Governor by George Gawler. Gawler was surprised by the apparent lack of progress and was disappointed that farming was still on a very small scale. He found that most of the colonists were still crowded together in Adelaide and that many preferred to speculate in land, rather than actually tilling it. Accordingly, he initiated a new period of expansion—so that during 1839 some 170,000 acres of land were surveyed and sold. By 1841 half-a-million acres had been made available for settlement, while a number of roads and other public works had been completed. Gawler's expansion was, of course, costly—and when he was replaced in 1841 by the new Governor, George Grey, he was accused of irresponsible over-spending. Certainly, by then the colony was suffering a crisis of confidence, capital and labour flowing from the colony, one Cornish emigrant later explaining that he had returned home to Saltash ". . . because of what he took to be the smash-up of South Australia when Governor Gawler's bills were dishonoured". Grey's stringent measures, however, coupled with the discovery of silver-lead deposits at Glen Osmond and a bumper harvest in 1842, put the colony back on its feet. It had been touch and go, nonetheless, and those that had arrived in South Australia at the height of the crisis had sent home first impressions contrasting strongly with those of the earlier settlers.

When James Sawle arrived in the colony in the early 1840s he found a settlement beset by gloom and pessimism, and it is not surprising that his reaction to this atmosphere—after all he had heard about South Australia—was one of dismay and anger. He wrote to his brother in Truro in angry and anguished tones, with not a good word to say about the colony. In retrospect, even his first day in Adelaide seemed to him to have been full of frustration and degradation. He wrote,

> After some delay and insolence on the part of the driver, you are brought into the midst of some very poor-looking wood huts; you ask what this place is, and you are told this is the Square. At a certain place your luggage is taken or rather thrown down, so that your little glass, or whatever else you have, is often knocked to pieces: After selecting what you can find of your things for the night, you ask where you are to lodge; you are directed to a wood hut, there may be a casement in the window-place, or there may not; however, there is no chimney for you to burn a little fire, and if there was it would be of no use to you for the night; you are now

exhausted with hunger and fatigue, your dear children crying with hunger and cold. You now enter a place, out of which, perhaps, two or three or more of a family have been carried dead, probably some of the old dirty garments remain, your floor is nothing but earth and dust; the smell from the burning of the oil and other causes is almost insufferable.

James Sawle was also scathing about the economic prospects of South Australia:

> . . . With regard to the abundance of labour, this is not true . . . . The prospects of the Colony are getting worse every day—those who were thought the richest men in the Colony, are now proved to be worth nothing, so that trade is at a standstill. Do not let any of my neighbours be deceived by false representations.

This reaction, however, was not typical of the views of most of the early Cornish settlers (Marmaduke Laurimer, it will be remembered, had exclaimed that "South Australia is one of the most beautiful countries in the world; all the splendid descriptions of it at home were strictly true . .")—one reason being that immigration had been halted abruptly as a result of the financial crisis, with only an unlucky few such as James Sawle arriving at the height of the depression. Moreover, the rapid development of the colony's mineral wealth, together with Grey's prudent housekeeping, ushered in a new period of expansion by the mid-1840s, and with it a new spirit of optimism.

Those Cornish immigrants who had arrived in the colony during the late 1830s and early 1840s formed an important part of embryonic Adelaide's population and, as many had known one another in Cornwall, or had forged friendships during the long voyages from Plymouth, they tended often to "stick together" once in the colony. Charles and Mary Dunn, from Piper's Pool in the parish of Trewen, for example, set up a blacksmith's business in Currie Street during 1839. Although they must have had any number of commercial relationships within the settlement, they chose their close friends from people they had known at home— there was Grace Sloggatt, and Mr Dinham and Mr Harvey (both from Camelford) who together ran a drapery and grocery shop in Adelaide. Other early residents of Currie Street included James and Ann Verco, and a Mr and Mrs Cornish. James and Ann hailed from Callington and had arrived in South Australia on 17 December 1840 in the "John Brightman". At home James had worked as a mason, and soon after his arrival in the colony he landed the important post of Foreman of the Works with the colonial Government, a position he was to hold until 1849 when he resigned to form his own business. James' closest and life-long friend was Philip Santo, from Saltash, who had also sailed in the "John Brightman" and was employed in Adelaide as a carpenter until appointed Clerk of the Works at the Burra Burra mine in 1849.

Two of early Adelaide's first Cornish settlers were James and Harriett Harvey (brother and sister) who arrived in December 1836 with Captain Hindmarsh onboard the "Buffalo". They set up a wheelwright's shop in Adelaide and erected the settlement's first lime-kiln. By 1843 they had also diversified into farming and blacksmithing. Another early arrival was James Grylls, from St Buryan, who in 1840 purchased land at Beaumont on the edge of the city. By 1844 he had 10 acres of wheat and one of barley under crop, and owned three cows and three pigs. From Tideford in the parish of St Germans came Samuel Sanders, who arrived at Port Adelaide in the "Recovery" in 1839. During that year he formed a mason's business in Weymouth Street, and was responsible for erecting several of Adelaide's early stone buildings. Another mason was Robert Dunstone, from Redruth, who arrived along with William Edwards, from Luxulyan, in the "Java" in February 1839. Other early arrivals included Joseph Allen from St Ewe—who set up a tentmaker's store in Leigh Street—and Samuel Coombe, from Lewannick, who found work as a brickmaker.

As land was gradually surveyed and made available, so the immigrants began to move beyond Adelaide to the surrounding plains. They found that the land on the Adelaide plains was relatively easy to clear (in 1842 the cost of clearing and preparing land in South Australia was £2 per acre, while in Tasmania it was £10), and in consequence the farming industry developed rapidly. In 1838 only 20 acres of wheat had been sown in the whole colony; by 1843 this figure had grown to a staggering 23,000 acres. Thereafter, the acreage continued to rise—wheat farming on the Adelaide plains, and in the colony as a whole, benefitting from the sudden upsurge in demand occasioned by the Victorian Gold Rush. In 1850, before the outbreak of the Rush, the South Australian wheat acreage stood at 41,807 acres. By 1857 the acreage had swollen to 175,865, South Australia producing more wheat per annum than any other Australian colony—she was by then "the granary of Australia".

One early settler on Adelaide's rural periphery who participated in this rapid expansion of wheat growing was Thomas King, from Landrake in East Cornwall. Thomas arrived in the colony in 1845 onboard the "Isabella Watson". He selected land outside the city in a district known as Morphett Vale, and set about clearing the land and establishing a farm. There were evidently other Cornish settlers in the vicinity, for in 1852 Thomas King married a local Cornish girl called Mary Ann Dungey who had arrived in the colony with her parents some years before.

Rather later settlers on the Adelaide plains, but of considerable interest, were members of the James family from West Cornwall. Charles James was born in Porthleven in 1839 and grew up to become a schoolmaster in that district. But in May 1865 he married 27-year old Emma Trevenen Gundry of St Hilary, and six weeks later the newly-weds set sail for South Australia in the "Electric". At first Charles worked as a grocer in Currie Street, but soon he was able to purchase land at East Marden, on the rich plains to the north-east of the city. There he established a market garden which, optimistically, he named "Lanhydrock" after the great house and estate of that name at home.

Charles James' cousin, Thomas, was born at St Hilary Churchtown in 1845. He, too, emigrated to South Australia in the "Electric" in 1865. On arrival in the colony he found work as a farm labourer, moving from farm to farm on the plains surrounding Adelaide, but before long he was able to join Charles and Emma at East Marden—purchasing some 17 acres of land there. By 1896 he was exporting oranges and grapes to London, and at the turn of the century was also trading with New Zealand.

Solomon Rowe James was another of that West Cornwall family. After a period of farming at Gilles Plains, just north of Adelaide, he returned home to Cornwall with the intention of purchasing farming property there. He found to his dismay, however, that many other Cornishmen were returning home from all corners of the world with the same idea. Unable to compete against these richer Cousin Jacks, he went back to South Australia in 1872, in the following year—perhaps as some kind of consolation—marrying a Cornish-born girl called Mary Broad. At the same time, he also commenced market gardening at East Marden, which was by then becoming a veritable James colony.

Two further members of the family were Charles' two brothers, William Wearne James (born in Gwithian in 1855) and Thomas White James (from St Hilary). During the 1870s they left Cornwall to work as coal miners at Ebbw Vale in South Wales. In 1876, however, they sailed for South Australia. After an abortive attempt to commence farming on Yorke Peninsula, which was then just being opened-up, they too took land at East Marden and the adjoining district of Beefacres. At first Thomas could only afford to buy two acres of land, starting out in this modest way as a horticulturalist, but before long he had expanded his property to some 30 acres—naming it "Kenwyn" after the parish in Cornwall. His brother William was initially the manager of a market garden at Beefacres, but after only 12 months purchased land at East Marden. There he grew citrus fruits, grapes, peaches, apricots and figs. He also became director of the important East End Market in Adelaide, his colleagues there including John Hammer, from St Austell, who was secretary of the Market, and George Phillips, from Redruth, who was then one of its leading merchants.

Curiously, the Cornish expertise in horticulture gave them an entrance into the colony's developing wine industry which, though associated very much with the Barossa Valley and the German settlers, could also learn from the Cornish experience. Two names stand out very clearly—those of Joseph Rowe Osborne and (particularly) William Thomas Angove. Osborne came from Truro, and in 1873 he arrived in South Australia to join the staff of Thomas Hardy & Sons, then up-and-coming grape-growers and wine merchants. He later became a senior member of the company as it grew from strength to strength, despite the rather amusing fact that he was a strict Methodist and teetotaller! Angove was, like Osborne, a Truro man. He trained initially as a doctor, graduating in 1875, and, following his marriage to Emma Carlyon in 1880, emigrated to South Australia. Once in Adelaide, he was employed by the Government to attend the city's destitute and poor. But he also leased five acres of land from a vigneron at Tea Tree Gully, a small settlement some ten miles north east of the capital, and entered the grape growing business. He was responsible for the naming of St Agnes, a village near Tea Tree Gully, and by 1903 had 100 acres in production in the district. His celebrated "Tregrehan Claret", named in honour of the Carlyon family of Tregrehan in Cornwall, is still a popular South Australian wine.

Increasingly, as the years passed, the Cornish became involved in every aspect of Adelaide society—in the economy, of course, but also in religion and in politics, as well as helping to mould the character of colonial cultural and social life. Cornishmen were world-famous as engineers and it is hardly surprising, if we may take one feature of local economic activity, that a number of Adelaide's prominent foundry owners and building contractors hailed from Cornwall. One builder of particular note was Nicholas Wallis Trudgen. Trudgen was born near Land's End in 1840 and arrived in South Australia some time during the 1850s. He spent a successful period on the Victorian and New South Wales goldfields in 1861–62 (the "Snowy River Rush") and returned to Adelaide wealthy enough to launch his own business. He was lucky from the start, and became one of Adelaide's foremost builders in the period 1865–92. His extensive premises were located in Wakefield Street, in the City, and he was responsible for the construction of many of Adelaide's characteristic suburban villas and for a number of important public buildings. Trudgen was for many years President of the influential Builders' and Contractors' Association, and in 1886 he became Mayor of the suburb of St Peters. He died tragically only a few years later, in May 1892, when he fell from a moving tram car and was fatally injured.

Trudgen may have been the best, but he had his imitators— Henry Dunstan from Camborne, John Penaluna, Richard Angwin, and Richard Barrett from Gunnislake who arrived in the colony in 1875 with his wife, Fanny Prideaux of Cargreen in the parish of Landulph, with the intention of setting-up a

34

building business. By the early 1880s "R. Barrett & Co.: Land Agents and Builders" was a prominent institution in Adelaide's Franklin Street. Andrew Jones & Co. was another Cornish-owned enterprise which achieved prominence in Adelaide in the early 1880s. The company had been established as early as 1855 and ran a foundry producing engineering components. Until 1882 it was a Government contractor for harbours and railways but, with the rise of the Broken Hill silver-lead-zinc mines in the 1880s, it turned its hand to the lucrative business of manufacturing Cornish boilers, pump engines and the like. In the same way, John Coumbe, another Cornishman, produced all sorts of equipment from milking machines to railway track at his "Coumbe Iron Works", while Thomas Grose—who was born in St Just-in-Penwith in 1837—was for many years foreman ironfounder at the Carron Iron Works, where he specialised in maritime repairs, enhancing Port Adelaide's reputation as a ship re-fitting centre.

All these tales of individual success and progress, of course, imply a certain degree of upward social mobility. Meryl Kuchel, in her valuable study, has demonstrated that of the 104 traceable Cornish passengers from the ships "Omega" (1851), "Hooghly" (1856), "Queen Bee" (1865) and "Salamanca" (1866), 23 maintained their previous occupational/social status, 72 were upwardly mobile (and able to maintain their improvement), while only nine were downwardly mobile. Other, less rigorous, studies conducted by students at the South Australian College of Advanced Education have also tended to confirm these findings, and suggest that the Cornish in South Australia were generally a socially upward mobile group. Perhaps the most extreme examples of this Cornish upward mobility were the fortunes of the Parsons, Rounsevell, and Bonython families, each of which became part of the Adelaide Establishment.

John Langdon Parsons was born at Botathan, near South Petherwin, in North Cornwall in 1837. He studied to be a Minister in the Baptist Church, and arrived in South Australia in 1863. He preached in several places in the colony (and also briefly in New Zealand) but soon aspired to a political career. In 1878 he was elected to the Adelaide Parliament, and had achieved Ministerial position by 1881. Thereafter he filled a number of

35

differing public posts, having already gained entrance to Adelaide "society" through his marriage to a granddaughter of the celebrated founding father, George Fife Angas. His son, Herbert Angas Parsons, perpetuated the upward mobility. He became a successful Adelaide lawyer, a Member of Parliament and a Government Minister. Like his father, he also married wisely—Elsie Bonython, a daughter of the great John Langdon Bonython, becoming his wife in 1900.

2. William Benjamin Rounsevell, Vice-President of the Cornish Association of South Australia at its foundation in 1890. Courtesy South Australian Archives.

The rise of the Parsons family in Adelaide was impressive, but perhaps even more so was that of the Rounsevells. In 1839 William Rounsevell was a common agricultural labourer at Tregrenna in the parish of Altarnun on Bodmin Moor. In that year, on the advice of Rowland Hill, he emigrated to South Australia, where he found employment as a police constable in Adelaide. By the time he had visited the Victorian diggings in the early 1850s he had already established a lucrative coaching business, "Rounsevell's" becoming a by-word in South Australia for efficient and reliable public transport over long distances. When, finally, William Rounsevell sold his company he made such a handsome profit that he was able to purchase a large country estate in the Barossa Valley, at the then enormous cost of £15,000, which he renamed "Corryton Park" to reflect an alleged family connection with the Corrytons of Pentillie Castle in Cornwall. His sons John and William Benjamin inherited his fortune on his death, later adding to it by purchasing further pastoral properties in far-flung corners of the colony. John died in 1902, but William survived until 1923 as a revered "old colonial" of Adelaide society, spending his days in his seaside villa "Tremere" or at the races where he operated under his "nomme de course", "W. B. Corryton".

The fortunes of the Bonython family were particularly noteworthy, for they represented the resurgence in Adelaide of a "bone fide" aristocratic line which in Cornwall had all but lost its former glory. In the sixteenth-century the Bonythons of Bonython and Carclew were amongst the principal landowners in the Hundred of Kerrier, but by the 1800s the sole remaining Cornish property was a small section of land at Trencreek in the parish of St Columb Minor, where Thomas Bonython worked as a cobbler. Sensing that they had little future in Cornwall, Thomas and his wife Ann (from Torpoint) went to Canada, where their son George Langdon Bonython was born. They later returned briefly to Cornwall but migrated to Adelaide in 1840, with George remaining in London to train as an architect. He married in 1844, and in 1848 in London *the* John Langdon Bonython was born, the family migrating to Adelaide in 1854.

Ten years later, in 1864, John Langdon Bonython was offered a junior position with the Adelaide *Advertiser* newspaper. Thereafter, his rise was meteoric. By 1879 he was a partner in the company, and by 1893 was sole owner. In 1884 he also took over the role of editor, a position he was to hold until his retirement in 1929. Under his guidance the *Advertiser* became the most

37

popular South Australian daily, eclipsing and finally absorbing the rival *Register*, and its success contributed to Bonython becoming almost certainly the wealthiest man in Adelaide. His son, John Lavington Bonython, born in 1876, was also involved closely with the *Advertiser*, and later became Mayor of Adelaide—the name Bonython being associated perhaps more than any other with the City in the years before the Second World War. Like the Rounsevells, the Bonythons were interested in their Cornish ancestors—but this was as much evidence of their deep attachment to Cornwall as it was of a desire to establish their aristocratic credentials.

The consolidation of the Cornish community in Adelaide in economic and social terms was also reflected in a certain cultural impact. During the 1840s Cornish Wrestling matches were popular in Adelaide, on one occasion in 1848 there being a grand "Cornwall v. Devonshire" match in Victoria Square attended by some 2,000 people. The strength of the "Cornwall and Devon Society" in the early 1850s was a mark of both the importance and distinctiveness of the Cornish (and Devon) community. It also reflected a certain ethnic consciousness, being a pressure group designed to win specific advantages for the Cornish community. Although many of its leading members were mine captains, the Society's committee also sported more than a sprinkling of Adelaide businessmen—Mr James Curnow of Grenfell Street, Mr John Painter of Gawler Place, Mr P. G. Moyle of Hindley Street, and so on.

The Cornish in Adelaide were actually quite sensitive about their reputation. In the *Register* newspaper in December 1848 William Stevens of Brown Street wrote that he wanted ". . . my brother Cornishmen (to) . . . know how disparagingly they are spoken of by some persons in Adelaide . . .". Stevens had visited a store in the city to sell a batch of shovels. But the storekeeper would have nothing to do with him and refused the merchandise, exclaiming that "There's not a d****d Cornishman in the colony that would use them, for they are too lazy." Stevens, understandably indignant, retorted that ". . . Cornishmen, 'one and all', are a match for any countryman any day, and more than a match for the best counter-jumper in the colony". Much later, in 1870, one Adelaide paper considered the Cornish community

38

significant enough to note that "Many Cornishmen in the province will read with regret of the . . . death . . . of Mr Cyrus Redding, one of the literary men of London. Born at Penryn, Cornwall, in 1785."

A minority of Cornish immigrants, typically the more middle class ones who had had the benefit of a reasonable education or had done particularly well in the colony, took a great interest in Cornwall and things Cornish. J. J. Pascoe, the Adelaide author, was one such fellow. In his celebrated *History of Adelaide*, published in 1901, he took every opportunity to praise the Cornish and their achievements. He wrote that ". . . a large Cornish element is found in the population of South Australia . . the energy and ambition of Cornishmen found for them prominence in colonial public affairs and commercial life". Richard Jagoe, a Truronian by birth and another of Adelaide's literary men, was shipping correspondent for several of the colony's newspapers in the latter part of the century, and his writings are full of Cornish allusions. He was at pains to assert his descent from the Trejagos of Fentongollan, in St Michael Penkevil, in an attempt to establish aristocratic connections.

John Langdon Bonython, inevitably, was the greatest of these Cornish enthusiasts. He spent many years studying his family's history and collecting Bonython relics and heirlooms, and in South Australia had two houses built which he named after ancient Bonython seats in Cornwall: Carclew and Carminow. Carclew was a strange "Gothic Revival" style building in North Adelaide, but Carminow—built in grey stone and situated amongst the trees on Mount Bonython in the Adelaide Hills— looked for all the world like a Tudor gentleman's house plucked straight from Cornwall. Indeed, Bonython incorporated a few stones from the Cornish Carminow in his building, and for its garden imported rhododendrons from Trelowarren. Alas, Carminow was razed to the ground in the dreadful bush-fires which swept through the Adelaide Hills in 1983.

A colleague and contemporary of John Langdon Bonython was James Penn Boucaut, one-time Premier, Supreme Court Judge, and Acting Governor. He was born at Mylor in 1831, and came to South Australia with his parents and brothers while still a youth but not before he had, to quote J. J. Pascoe, ". . . received

3a. Sir John Langdon Bonython, Vice-President of the Cornish Association at its foundation (courtesy South Australian Archives). 3b. The "Bonython Flagon"—a Bonython heirloom illustrated in the *Supplement to the Western Antiquary* of March 1882.

THE BONYTHON FLAGON

(*Described in the Bonython Notes*).

Engraved from a photograph by the MELBOURNE PHOTO-GRAPHIC COMPANY, 76, Rundle Street, Adelaide, S.A., for the owner of the Flagon, MR. JOHN LANGDON BONYTHON, Adelaide, South Australia.

those delightful impressions found in quaint legend and hoary tradition so dear to the heart of every true Cornishman." Boucaut attributed many of his attitudes and dispositions to his Cornish background, and like Bonython developed a consuming passion for Cornwall and its heritage. This found its ultimate expression in 1892 when he revisited Cornwall. He made a special pilgrimage to Mylor Church, writing with some emotion that "Though I was not seven when I left this part—now alas! fifty three years ago, and have never seen it since—I knew every step of the way and at once detected the alterations, which were few". Quite paradoxically, for he had played a significant part (as we shall see) in the expansion of South Australia, he was sad that the colonies ". . . with their richer mines, have beaten poor old Cornwall, which now seeks amends by growing vegetables for the Londoners . . . ."

Back in South Australia, Boucaut joined forces with John Langdon Bonython to help found the "Cornish Association of South Australia", which was in some respects an echo of the earlier "Cornwall and Devon Society" but was principally a social and cultural institution rather than a political pressure group. Sir Arthur Quiller-Couch's *Cornish Magazine* ran a lengthy article, complete with photographs, describing the Cornish connections of both Boucaut and Bonython, and reports of the foundation of the Association found their way into a number of Cornish and colonial newspapers. The inaugural meeting of the Association was at a banquet in Adelaide Town Hall on 21 February 1890. The yearly subscription was five shillings, membership being open to all who were ". . . Cornishmen by birth, descent or long residence". Boucaut was the first Chairman and President, and Bonython and W. B. Rounsevell became the two Vice-Presidents. At the inaugural meeting it was declared with some pride that ". . . South Australians and Cornishmen are synonomous terms . . .", the aims of the Association being to:

> . . . assist in forming or maintaining friendly intimacy and interest among those who are of Cornish birth or extraction, to keep alive Cornish customs; to encourage the settlement of that colony (sic!) in this; and to disseminate information regarding South Australia in Cornwall; and to assist any who may be in difficulty or distress.

41

4. Sir James Penn Boucaut, Chairman and President of the Cornish Association of South Australia at its foundation. As Premier of the Colony in the 1870s, he pioneered a vigorous policy of frontier expansion. Courtesy South Australian Archives.

One especially significant aspect of the Cornish cultural impact in early Adelaide was religious nonconformity, particularly Methodism. Cornish colonists had been attracted by South Australia's "liberal dissenting" atmosphere—the spirit of civil liberty, socio-economic opportunity and religious equality—and, once settled in the colony, helped to consolidate and further develop Adelaide's dissenting reputation. As John Reynolds has written,

> The social environment of South Australia seems to have favoured these hard-working, individualistic church-going people (the Cornish) who found themselves removed from a land of squire and parson in what historian Douglas Pike has named a "Paradise of Dissent".

The first Methodist service in South Australia was held in early 1837 at Glenelg, where Hindmarsh had landed, by Edward Stephens—one of the celebrated Stephens brothers. Within a few years chapels had been erected—Samuel Bray from Falmouth wrote in 1839 that he attended a chapel as big as Budock chapel and that one the size of Penryn chapel was almost completed—and by 1843 there were in addition regular Methodist meetings being held in 16 private homes and 30 other preaching stations in Adelaide and environs. At first, the Wesleyans seem to have been the strongest denomination, but there was also a group of New Connexion Methodists who were, as Pike wrote, ". . . tortured for a time by the attentions of a Cornishman from Truro, James Sawle . . .", the author of several fiery letters to Cornish and South Australian newspapers.

Amongst the early Cornish settlers were a number of Bible Christians. Although they were active mostly at the Kapunda and Burra Burra copper mines, there were several who settled in Adelaide itself. In the suburb of Brompton, for example, lived Samuel Coombe from Lewannick. It was in his house that the Rev. James Way, one of the two trained Bible Christian ministers sent to the colony in 1850 by the Bible Christian Missionary Society, preached his first sermon in South Australia. Neighbours of Samuel Coombe at Brompton included Mrs Frances Fry, another Bible Christian from Lewannick, and her brother, a certain James Harry. At home, in Cornwall and Devon, the Bible Christian Connexion looked on with amazement and delight as their denomination grew rapidly from strength to strength in the new colony. In 1905 F. W. Bourne described the emotional scenes at Shebbear at the so-called "Weeping Conference" of 1850 when the Rev. James Way and the Rev. James Rowe (from Penzance) were selected for South Australia:

> . . . standing in circle on the platform, (they) joined hands in solemn covenant that they would remain one in heart when oceans rolled between them. Fervent ejaculatory prayer and loud shouts of praise continually ascended to heaven. The weeping, the rejoicing were general.

The Primitive Methodists, too, attracted support from the

Cornish community in early Adelaide. Cornishmen were amongst the congregation when a Primitive Methodist chapel was opened in Light Square, in Adelaide, on 11 October 1840, and as early as 1841 a long article on the colony appeared in the *Primitive Methodist Magazine*. Only a few years later, in 1848, one Cornish settler, Nicholas Brokenshire, could enthuse over what he saw as the successful "civilising" effect of Primitive Methodism:

> On my arrival here I used to see many children belonging to the white population, who, in their manners, bore too striking a resemblance to those of the poor black natives—running about the bush and over the hills barefoot, and with scarcely any clothing; and, apparently, neither fearing God, nor regarding man. But now I have the pleasure, every Sabbath morning, of meeting from 55 to 60 of these dear children in the home of prayer . . . .

In the following year, 1849, this assessment was echoed in the *Primitive Methodist Magazine*, which commented that "In Adelaide and surrounding villages we are steadily progressing, both in numbers and piety".

Of the other nonconformist sects in early Adelaide, the Church of Christ (or "Scotch Baptists") attracted a number of Cornishmen into its ranks—notably Philip Santo, from Saltash, and James Verco, from Callington. Santo joined the "Scotch Baptists" on arrival in Adelaide, and H. R. Taylor—in assessing the importance of Santo's contribution in the early religious life in the colony—wrote that "To this kindly Christian man may be attributed much of the success of laying the foundations of the cause of primitive Christianity in South Australia". Santo and Verco were instrumental in erecting the colony's first Church of Christ, in Adelaide's Franklin Street, the two men contributing more than £10 towards the total cost of £90 and actually building the chapel themselves (both were tradesmen in the building industry). The chapel was opened in January 1846, the *Register* newspaper remarking that ". . . the body of Christians, commonly known as Scotch Baptists, but who eschewing all denominational distinction, call themselves the Church of Christ . . ." had commenced worshipping in their new chapel with only the minimum of ceremony and publicity, this being in accordance with their ". . . retiring and unostentatious habits".

44

The Baptists, too, had Cornish members—the most significant being the Rev. John Langdon Parsons, from Botathan, near South Petherwin. He was for many years minister at the Tynte Street chapel in North Adelaide. His sermon notes have survived from those early days, and their content and style give the impression of a learned, serious, intellectual theologian—a far cry from the stereotype of the unsophisticated, "Bible-thumping", hell-fire-and-brimstone Cornish preacher. His message was not only the "repent and be saved" upon which many dwelt so extensively, but went deeper to convey, for example, the importance and meaning of Christ's words "It is finished" at the Crucifixion, and the especial significance of the imagery and language of St John's Gospel.

The importance of the Cornish contribution to nonconformity in Adelaide and environs is reflected in the obituary columns of the local Methodist magazines (such as the *Australian Christian Commonwealth, the Christian Weekly and Methodist Journal,* and the *South Australian Primitive Methodist*) at the turn of the century, in which there were glowing accounts of the work performed by early Cornish settlers. There was James Reseigh from Newlyn who was a stalwart of Brompton Wesleyan chapel; William Short from Quethiock who helped build the first chapel at Enfield; John Tremelling from Crowan who was a Primitive Methodist at Dry Creek; John Magor from Gwennap, another Primitive Methodist; Samuel Prior from St Austell who helped the Congregationalists, Primitive Methodists and Wesleyans build their chapels at Glenelg and Brighton; and Thomas Trevail of the North Adelaide Primitive Methodists. The list is seemingly endless.

But despite all this, the development of the nonconformist denominations in Adelaide, with their strong Cornish influence, was not always easy or straight-forward. Early South Australia earned a reputation as a haven of religious freedom but this was soon threatened through the implementation of financial State-aid to the various Churches. The nonconformists, already used to raising their own funds and convinced of the moral value of self-help, resented this State interference in their affairs and in 1841 founded the "Society for the Preservation of Religious Freedom in the Province". Its chairman was Edward Stephens, who had conducted the first Methodist service in the colony, and one of its leading committee members was the Truronian James Sawle. The Society was supported strongly by John Stephens, through the pages of his *Register*, and the threat was averted. It re-emerged, however, in 1846 when a system of State-aid was again proposed (and indeed later implemented). Edward Stephens was in the forefront of the renewed attempts to fight State interference, and in the colony's Legislative Council he found a strong ally in Penzance-born George Marsden Waterhouse—another son of a Methodist minister. Largely through their actions State aid was abandoned in 1851, and when full self-government was granted in 1857 there was no mention of a relationship between Church and State: South Australia became thus the first British territory to break the Church and State link and achieve full equality for all denominations. It was to their great credit that Cornishmen had been involved in the struggle.

Cornishmen also became involved in other political struggles, particularly after self-government in 1857. The major Cornish contribution, however, was from the mining towns—as detailed in *The Cornish Miner in Australia*—although there was a handful of Adelaide men who did become politically involved. George Marsden Waterhouse was one such activist. Born in Penzance in 1824, he arrived in early South Australia as a young man and was quick to involve himself in local political issues—not the least of which was the religious freedom debate. That his father was a Yorkshireman might lead us to question his "Cornish credentials", but he was brought up in a strict Methodist atmosphere (his father was a Wesleyan minister) and was educated at the Wesleyan College at Kingswood, near Bristol—a Methodist mining community, socially not unlike Cornwall itself. His politics, too, reflected the Cornish inheritance, and when he was elected to the Legislative Council in 1851 he advocated liberal measures such as the abolition of State aid to religion, an extended suffrage, vote by secret ballot, the abolition of the Imperial veto on local legislation, a curtailment of the Governor's financial prerogative, triennial elections, and popular education. In the debate on the Constitution for self-government he opposed the concept of a nominated Upper House. He first became Premier of South Australia in 1861, and both then and in later Premierships in the colony and in New Zealand he was—as the *Australian Dictionary of Biography* puts it—". . . interested above all in economic development and the freeing of trade . . .".

Philip Santo and James Verco were two other liberal nonconformists who became involved in early Adelaide's political scene, Santo serving in Parliament from 1860 to 1882 (five years as Commissioner of Public Works) and Verco serving from 1860 until 1865. But perhaps the greatest Parliamentary product of Adelaide's "Paradise of Dissent" was James Penn Boucaut and his bold programme of reform which, as the *Primitive Methodist Quarterly Review* observed as early as 1890, would never have been formulated—let alone implemented—if the correct social conditions had not first been moulded in the colony by the early settlers. Paradoxically, Boucaut was an Anglican, but politically he was a natural ally of the dissenters and, as was reported in the *Bible Christian Magazine* in 1876, he had on numerous occasions ". . . wanted to express my sympathy towards the Nonconformist churches, partly from my own natural feelings and greatly from old family associations".

Boucaut's intimate links with the miners' trade union at Moonta have been explored elsewhere by the writer, but it is useful here to glimpse at other aspects of his political career. He was first elected to the House of Assembly (the lower House) in 1861, shortly forming a personal political alliance with Santo and Verco. In 1862 he was surprisingly defeated in his efforts to be returned as a Member for East Adelaide, but he again entered the political arena in 1865 when he successfully contested West Adelaide. In this, his second session in Parliament, he directed his attentions to winning various forms of relief for drought-stricken pastoralists in the Far North of the colony—demonstrating an interest in frontier expansion which would later develop into a significant political enthusiasm. In 1866 Boucaut became Premier for a short period, but in 1868 he again lost his seat. However, in the same year he was returned as Member for Burra Burra and, although briefly out of Parliament for a few months during 1870–71, he emerged in the period 1872–75 as the leader of the Opposition groups in the House of Assembly. His enemies branded him a "Red Republican" on account of his progressive views, but in October 1874 he introduced his famous railway scheme and shortly after became Premier for a second time.

As head of Government, Boucaut pressed on with his courageous and far-sighted plans for the expansion of South Australia's frontiers of settlement, planning 13 new railways to traverse the colony and penetrate its more distant corners. Other public works, designed to facilitate the process of agricultural expansion, were also initiated, and Boucaut advocated increased immigration to help populate the new areas thus opened up. His schemes, however, were very expensive and were to be financed by borrowing £2,200,000, the interest on which was to be met through increased taxation. This aspect of the plan, together with its radical, sweeping nature, met stiff resistance from the conservative Legislative Council (the upper house) and was thus rejected on two occasions. Losing the confidence of the lower house as a result of his failure, Boucaut was replaced as Premier by a politician named Cotton who then proceeded to press ahead with much of Boucaut's planned legislation. When Boucaut regained the Premiership in October 1877 several stages of his railway programme had already been implemented, and he had the personal satisfaction of introducing the later stages. These new lines of communication were indeed important in opening-up the hitherto uninhabited, remote parts of the colony, and Boucaut has been duly recognised as one of South Australia's more important Premiers.

James Penn Boucaut, then, was not only a significant figure in the consolidation of the Cornish community within Adelaide itself, but also was intimately concerned with the projection of the colony's agricultural frontier. For by the mid-1870s, when Boucaut was at the zenith of his powers, the settlement frontier had already moved well beyon the confines of Adelaide and environs—into the Hills and beyond, to the plains and rolling Central Hill Country of the Lower and Mid-North, into the South East, onto Yorke Peninsula, and now, with faltering steps, into the Far North district of the southern Flinders Ranges. Cornish men and women, as might be expected, were part of this process of expansion and, having glimpsed their role in the establishment and growth of Adelaide, it is appropriate for us to follow them into the depths of rural South Australia.

# CHAPTER 4

## *Expanding Horizons*

The expansion outwards from the immediate Adelaide district took the settlers to three new areas, to the range of hills running down the eastern side of the city, to the coastal strip to the south of Adelaide, and to the plains lying to the north of the capital. In the Adelaide Hills, Cornish families were amongst the first settlers. By 1840 there were already 2,036 acres of land enclosed in the Mount Barker–Strathalbyn area of the Hills, 646 of which were under cultivation. A traveller by the name of John Dunn visited the district at about that time, noting that ". . . there were only four persons settled where the town of Nairne now stands . . .", one of whom was a Mr Hilman, ". . . a Cornish carpenter".

Soon Hilman was joined by other arrivals from Cornwall, and before long a sizeable Cornish community had been created in that part of the Hills. John Rundle purchased land at Mount Barker in 1840, and his neighbours there included a Mr Rendell from Linkinhorne, George and Grace Venning from Altarnun, and other Cornish settlers by the names of William Tonkin, Joseph Bull and Edward Hender. Clearly, they were all well known to one another and enjoyed a fairly close relationship. This was reflected in the letters written home by some of these settlers so that, for example, William Rendell of Linkinhorne received a letter from his son at Mount Barker explaining that,

> William Tonkin has a farm to himself of 40 acres, and six good working oxen. Joseph Bull has a section of 80 acres and six working bullocks . . . William Tonkin has had this year about 400 bushels of wheat, and will have more next year.

The Medland family from St Blazey was also friendly with William Tonkin, Peter Medland writing home that,

> Mr Tonkin's son William, we hear is doing well, he has got forty acres of cultivated land in the district of Mount Barker, about thirty miles from the city, he lives near the old John Rundle, and had got 3 children and we believe are quite well.

In the nearby township of Strathalbyn, two early settlers were

William Rowe and Richard Trenouth. Rowe was born in Truro in 1820 and emigrated to Victoria during the Gold Rush days. By 1855, however, he had arrived in South Australia and in that year he opened his "Britannia Foundry" in Strathalbyn. In those days his foundry was by far the most important commercial enterprise in the township, and Rowe's services as a wheelwright and manufacturer of agricultural implements were much in demand from the surrounding rural communities. Richard Trenouth was born at Holmbush, near St Austell, in 1830 and arrived at Strathalbyn in 1857. He established a building trade and was responsible for erecting many of the little town's fine buildings, notably the tower of St Andrew's Presbyterian Church.

5. Typical Hills scenery, near Mount Barker. From William Harcus, *South Australia*, 1876.

As the communities became thus more settled and more permanent in nature and appearance, so the colonists in the Hills could look upon their achievements with a sort of reflective pride. They felt rather pleased with themselves, and a number wrote home to no doubt envious friends and relatives in the Old Country, explaining (some might say boasting about) their success in South Australia. One such letter found its way into the

January 1848 issue of the *South Australian News* newspaper, a detailed description by one T. Sawle from Truro—intended for his friend, Thomas Crocker of the same town—of his farming activities in the colony. He wrote that,

> . . . the particular spot on which I live is the most beautiful and lovely of which you can form any conception. My house bears the designation Park Cottage; the soil is the richest you ever saw . . . I have cropped from two to ten acres these two years. My wheat crops I consider to be very good, yielding about 35 bushels per acre the first year, and this without English farming: ploughed once, and seed sown immediately, drew the harrow over it three times last December, which is generally the time of our harvest here; I reaped a self-sown crop that which grew from that which was shed in gathering the crop the year before. I could not procure cattle so much as to harrow my land, yet I doubt not I shall realize 25 bushels per acre, of as good a sample of wheat as ever grew. My English barley crop was not so good. The Cape barley will yield most plentifully, but it is of little value, fit only for pigs and cattle; but the English barley is just as high as wheat. I put in about 14 or 16 yards of potatoes last season, and have just taken them out, they are good in quality, but fall far short of an English crop—but we regard them as a luxury. I do not consider this a proper trial, because the land was not properly worked. Potatoes are very cheap with us now, selling at 8lbs for 6d. Wheat has been of very little value, at from 2s to 2s 6d per bushel, but it is now on the advance, somewhere about 3s 3d.

In a Cornwall still attempting to recover from the blights and poverty of the "Hungry Forties", the calm, easy, almost complacent tone of Sawle's remarks must have seemed incredible, and it was hardly surprising that the *West Briton* should note that "High rents, heavy rates, and obnoxious and impoverishing taxes are driving some of the best of our agriculturalists to climes where these demons of robbery and ruin are unknown".

Another district to attract Cornish settlers was the area around Chain of Ponds, further north from Mount Barker. The village of Millbrook, in that locality, was named after Millbrook (near Torpoint) in Cornwall by John Tippett, who hailed from that town, and the nearby "Trevale" property was thus named by its owner, Cornishman James Trestrail. Kersbrook, in the same vicinity, grew into a rather typical Hills community, almost idyllic in its sylvan setting amongst the eucalyptus trees, but was originally a single farmstead—owned by one John Bowden. Bowden was born on 31 July 1798 at Kersbrook in the parish of Linkinhorne, and in September 1821 married Agnes Turner of South Petherwin. Together they lived at Coads Green in the parish of North Hill until sailing for South Australia in September 1837 in the "Red Admiral". John's younger brother Jacob, from nearby Fivelanes, also accompanied them, and once in Adelaide opened a herbalist's shop in Gilles Street. John found work initially as manager of the South Australian Company's dairy in Adelaide, but in 1841 he and Agnes purchased land near Chain of Ponds, calling their farm "Kersbrook" after his birthplace. By 1844 John Bowden had 800 head of sheep, 62 cattle, one horse, 13 pigs, 16 acres of wheat, 8 acres of barley, together with plots of oats, maize, potatoes, and a fruit garden!

This prosperous, largely self-sufficient, existence would have been typical of the experience of many Hills settlers, though one should not under-estimate the immense hard work, long hours of toil, and initial financial difficulties that most colonists had to endure in clearing their land and establishing their homes. Social life, as was so often the case, centred around the religious institutions and, as might be expected, the Cornish were keen to play leading roles in bringing nonconformity to the newly opened-up districts. Rural expansion was, of course, a constant—if sometimes rather erratic—process, and the Methodists in particular realised the necessity of keeping their own development abreast of this growth. In June 1855 a Primitive Methodist wrote to the Conference in Britain, requesting further Missionaries for the colony:

> . . . some of our brethren are leaving our stations, and going into the Bush, where new townships are being laid out; and they say 'Come after us; we need you in the Bush'; and we cannot attend these calls. We shall be very glad to hear that two other missionaries are on their way here . . . .

But when the parent bodies in Britain did not have the funds or the personnel to give assistance, the pioneers in bush districts such as the Adelaide Hills took it upon themselves to begin the

Missionary work, and therein lay the strength of Methodism in South Australia. In the Mount Barker Wesleyan Circuit, for example, George Venning and his brother John were enthusiastic local preachers, while Edward Hender donated the land upon which their chapel was built and ran the Sunday School. The Primitive Methodists also erected a chapel at Mount Barker, their congregation there including a certain Harriet Davies from Gwennap.

Turning to the coastal districts to the south of Adelaide, Willunga and Aldinga were two areas opened up for agricultural purposes as early as 1838 and which consequently became one of the first regions to be farmed extensively in South Australia. With the abolition of the Corn Laws in Britain in 1846, and the later jump in demand occasioned by the Victorian Gold Rush, the Willunga area became an important wheat-growing district and indeed remained the colony's principal cereal producer until eclipsed by the Mid-North and Far-North in the 1860s and 1870s. The first settler at Aldinga was John Pengilly, a Cornishman, while another Cornish colonist—Abraham Pethick—was the first to construct a permanent house there. Pethick arrived in South Australia in 1839 in the "Cleveland", selecting land at Aldinga and naming his property "Bowithick" after his old farm on Bodmin Moor. He had the distinction of being one of the first to export wheat from South Australia, a fact that earned him a well-deserved place in the biographical section of H. T. Burgess' *The Cyclopedea of South Australia* which was published in 1907 and described the careers of notable "old colonials".

Other Cornish settlers in the area included George Sara from Perranwell, John Orchard from Wendron, James Binney, and James Sibley Jacobs who ran the Willunga general-store for many years. Honor Vellanoweth emigrated to South Australia from Cornwall with her parents sometime before December 1841. In that month she married Thomas Marshall, a Lincolnshire farmer who had purchased land near Willunga. Honor wrote home in January 1842 to her friend, Elizabeth Rowe of St Ives, explaining how she and her husband were building their house and acknowledging gratefully that they had had already a bumper harvest of wheat. She added that they also owned some cattle and intended to grow vegetables as well. Interestingly, for her comment provides a window into one of South Australia's least known Cornish communities, she mentioned that her brothers—Bennett and William—were employed in local quarries where, she said, "They have a good sale of slate".

Closer inspection reveals that a great many other Cornishmen found work in the Willunga slate quarries. In their hey-day these quarries employed as many as 100 workmen, and the existence of a "Cornwall Inn" in Willunga township was an indication of a strong Cornish influence in the workforce and in the settlement as a whole. Slate had been discovered at Willunga in 1840 and by 1841 it was already an important export commodity. In 1845 there were three principal quarries being worked in the district and, although there was a decline in the industry in the late 1840s, the 1850s and 1860s were periods of continuing prosperity, while the years 1875 to 1900 witnessed a veritable slate boom.

For much of the second half of the last century there were four quarries in operation—Martin's, Bastian's, Bangor and the delightfully named Delabole. Martin's Willunga Quarry was opened in the early 1850s by Thomas Williams and Thomas Polkinghorne, two Cornishmen, but was soon purchased from them by Thomas Martin. Martin was born in Cornwall in 1825 and emigrated to South Australia in the 1840s while still a youth. On arrival in the colony he heard of the slate discoveries and made his way to Willunga, finding work in the quarries and later taking over his own enterprise from Williams and Polkinghorne. One of his employees there was a St Dennis man, Richard Best, and prior to 1855 he leased out a portion of his property to James Kernick, W. B. Male and William Cobbledick who were, as the *Register* newspaper put it, three ". . . experienced Cornish stone dressers . . .". Martin continued to work his quarry until his death in 1900, and his son carried his business on until operations were suspended in 1912.

Thomas Martin had also had a share in Bastian's quarry, which had been opened by a Cornishman called Sampson Bastian. In time, Bastian became sole owner of the quarry, Martin having decided to sell back his share, and for more than

40 years his workings afforded employment for a dozen local residents. When the section they had leased from Thomas Martin collapsed in 1856, Kernick, Male and Cobbledick decided that they too would open their own quarry. It is interesting that Kernick came originally from Trevena, in the heart of Cornwall's slate country, and it is likely that Male and Cobbledick were also North Cornishmen. Curiously, though, they named their quarry "Bangor", after the celebrated slate district of North Wales. The trio remained in business until 1884 when they sold out to George Sara, who in turn sold the quarry to a certain Harry Richards.

"Delabole" quarry was opened in the early 1840s by Sampson Dawe, who, of course, named the venture after the great Delabole Quarry in North Cornwall. In 1855 John Allen, yet another Cornishman, acquired the property and, although he lost control of the enterprise briefly from 1860 to 1872, by the early 70s he was back at the reins and providing high quality slate for important public buildings such as the Adelaide General Post Office, the Adelaide Town Hall and the City Museum. Dawe's early confidence, reflected in his bold choice of name, was certainly justified and the quarry continued in use until closure in 1903.

Adjacent to Delabole Quarry was the Delabole Quarry Village where many of the Cornishmen lived (among them Henry Waters, Simon Sibly and William Herring from Tintagel), a settlement large enough to have its own Wesleyan Chapel. As elsewhere, many of the Cornish at Willunga were Methodists and the local farmers and quarrymen strongly supported the various chapels. By 1859, for example, the local Bible Christian chapel was thriving, surnames as ever being a clue to Cornish involvement—Trenaman, Male, Bastian, Sibley, Harris, Thomas, Williams, Sanders, Pearce, Polkinghorne, Osborne, Nicholls, and Vanstone. The Wesleyans, too, had the support of local Cornish settlers. Elizabeth Cornelius, who was born in Cornwall in 1816, had been an Anglican at home but on her arrival at Willunga in 1857 decided to join the Wesleyan chapel. William Herring was a Wesleyan class-leader and local preacher.

At Yankalilla, a few miles further south from Willunga, there was another cluster of Cornish families. Alexander Sampson was one of the earliest colonists in the district. He called his farm "Carn Brea", after the hill and village of that name in Cornwall, and his daughter Jesse married another Cornishman in the area, Charles Sanders from St Neot. James Holman, from South Petherwin, arrived in South Australia in 1839 and commenced farming at Yankalilla, while in the following year—1840—the first of the Tonkin family from Penzance, Enoch and his wife, settled in the same district. Between 1840 and 1849 the rest of the family—James, John, and John Charles—emigrated to the colony, James marrying a local girl named Prudence Trenouth (also from Penzance) in 1856. James became a Wesleyan Sunday School teacher and a class-leader, while as late as November 1904, after her death, Prudence was still remembered with affection as ". . . a leading light in the Christmas Festival"! Such comments, perhaps, written many years after the first settlement, give a misleadingly "cosy" picture of the early colonist's lot (what fun the Yankalilla Christmas Festival must have been!). By contrast, poor John Cornish, from Helston, could only look back with regret to those harsh and dangerous days when his coasting ketch, the "Cowrie", was wrecked during a stormy passage from its Yankalilla base to Kangeroo Island.

Some twenty miles east of Yankalilla, on the mouth of Lake Alexandrina and the Murray, lay Hindmarsh Island. Here John Tremain arrival from Cornwall with his wife Jane in 1852. They farmed on the Island until 1882 when they moved to a larger property at Mundulla in the south-east of the colony, near the Victorian border. Their son, William "Nugget" Tremain, became a sheep-shearer of some repute in both South Australia and Victoria, and R. A. C. and T. E. Knowling's charming description of Nugget's abilities and character show the extent to which the Cornish could become ingrained totally in Australian country life. Nugget, they say,

> . . . was known wherever sheep were shorn, and his name became a household word in almost every State. As a humorist he was second to none, and shearing sheds were always considered fortunate if he was included in their team. While away in the shearing season he always looked on the bright side of every situation, and could see a silver lining in every cloud. He had the happy knack of creating a cheerful atmosphere in any camp.

56

Elsewhere in the south-east of the colony there was also a sprinkling of Cornish settlers. There was, for example, Richard Jewell. He was born in Cornwall in 1829 and arrived in South Australia in 1856. He worked as a farm labourer for sixteen years before purchasing his own farm at Strathalbyn and later moving to a more extensive property at Narracoorte, in the south east, where he owned 500 acres of land. To small-holders at home in Cornwall such acreages seemed beyond comprehension, but in Australia they were not likely to raise many eyebrows—Charles Colwill, another Cornishman, farmed some 700 acres in the Narracoorte district, while Samuel Skewes from Cury owned 580 acres at Millicent, named "Nantithet" after his birthplace in Cornwall.

The plains lying to the north of Adelaide were, like the districts surrounding Willunga and Aldinga, opened up for settlement at an early date and attracted numerous Cornish settlers who came as both farmers and artizans. The settlement of Salisbury lay upon the plains immediately north of Adelaide, and further north still was the township of Gawler. Named, of course, after the colony's Governor, Gawler grew up around the confluence of the North and South Para rivers, a natural choice for a settlement in that district. By 1839 part of the township had already been surveyed and laid-out, and it expanded quickly—soon to become, after Adelaide, the colony's second settlement. It acted, as its founders had hoped, as a gateway to the vast tracts of land to the north, and its social and cultural life earned the town the flattering title of the "Athens of South Australia". As in the case of Adelaide's own expansion, the growth of Gawler township acted as a catalyst to the development of the surrounding countryside, and soon the Gawler Plains were fairly covered with farms and small settlements.

John and Elizabeth Magor were early arrivals from Cornwall on the Plains near Salisbury. They called their farm "Carclew", and the settlement emerged as an important focal point for other Cornish folk arriving in the district. Ezekial Johns came from Redruth, and he and his Cornish friends—William Roberts, Peter Rowe, and of course John Magor—set about building Carclew Primitive Methodist Chapel. The Goodman family came to South Australia in 1848 from Ponsanooth. Nicholas

57

Goodman set up a blacksmith's shop in Salisbury township, and after 1852 went into partnership with his son to farm in the locality. Another Salisbury family was the Pedlers, from Twelveheads in the parish of Kea. They arrived in the colony in 1838 in the "Red Admiral", William Pedler working as a cobbler until April 1850 when he purchased his 135 acre farm, "Trevalsa", near Salisbury.

The major influx of Cornish people onto the Gawler Plains occurred in the 1850s. There were some who had been in the colony for a number of years and who, following some success on the Victorian Diggings, had decided to turn their hands to farming. Such was the experience of William Worden, born in Cornwall in 1826, who had worked as a copper miner in the Burra Burra mine, or of James Harvey—another Burra miner—who returned to South Australia in 1858 rich enough to purchase 186 acres at Roseworthy, just north of Gawler township.

6. A display of farming implements in use on the Gawler Plains. From William Harcus, *South Australia*, 1876.

Most of the 1850s arrivals, however, came from Cornwall

directly. There was James Mitchell from Altarnun, Henry Secomb from Helston and his wife Margaret from St Keverne, Reuben Magor from Gwennap, Richard Nottle from Lostwithiel, and Thomas Bartlett from Saltash. Of particular interest were William Henry Gartrell and his son Edwin, from Roseworthy near Camborne. They arrived in the colony in the "Trafalgar" in 1847, and in April 1855 selected land in the Hundred of Mudla Wirra on the Five Mile Plain north of Gawler. William named his farm, predictably enough, "Roseworthy", and worked the property until his death in 1864 when Edwin sold-out and moved into Gawler township. Just as John and Elizabeth Magor had acted as the focal points of a small Cornish community at Salisbury, using the Primitive Methodist Chapel at Carclew as a means of drawing the settlers together, so the Gartrells built a Primitive Methodist Chapel at Roseworthy for the benefit of others in that area. It was at the chapel that young Edwin met his wife-to-be, a Cornish lass, a certain Miss Skewes.

If the Primitive Methodists were active, then so too were the Bible Christians! Chapels were especially thick on the ground in their Gawler Circuit, each one identified by its intensely evocative Biblical name—Ebenezer, Zoar, Salem, Bethesda, Enon, Hephizibah, Zion, Elim, Emmanuel, Bethany. Equally telling were the names of the Connexion's local members, many subscribers in the Gawler Circuit in 1859 sporting Cornish surnames, among them Edgecombe, Mitchell, Hawke, Matthews, Philp, Varcoe, Dennis, Hawker, Symonds, Hick, and Leane. Christopher Temby, born in Crowan (where, as one Methodist obituary put it, he was ". . . hushed as an infant with the songs of Zion . . ."), was amongst the first to worship in the Bible Christian chapel at Gawler River where his wife, Sarah Glasson from Stithians, was also active. Richard Stephens, who had had considerable experience as a local preacher at Newlyn East before emigrating to South Australia, was another stalwart. James Mitchell, from Altarnun, settled at Gawler River in 1850 and it was in his home that the Rev. Samuel Keen, sent to the colony by the Bible Christian Conference in 1852, conducted services until the Salem Chapel on Gawler Plains was completed. Such, of course, was the strength of Methodism—and particularly its Cornish brands—

and which allowed religious nonconformity to keep abreast of colonial expansion. It was a measure of their numerical strength in the colony, and of Methodism as a central strand of the Cornish identity in the last century, that Cornish men and women played such a significant role in the growth of the various Methodist denominations in rural South Australia.

7. Reaping on Gawler Plains. From William Harcus, *South Australia*, 1876.

Gawler township itself, like early Adelaide, also exhibited all the signs of a strong Cornish influence. The Methodists were active, of course, but Cornish Wrestling was very popular (J. Wills was the Gawler champion in 1859) and a vigorous Gawler Branch of the Cornish Association of South Australia was formed in the 1890s. In particular, Gawler Town was (and still is) connected closely in the public mind with the Martin family from Stithians in West Cornwall. James Martin was hailed in his day as "The Father of Gawler" (he is thus described in E. H. Coombe's *History of Gawler* of 1910) and was born near the old Stithians Foundry (which had been built by his grandfather) on 23 April 1821. As a boy he was employed as a wheelwright in Truro, but was later apprenticed as an engineer at the mighty

Tresavean copper mine. At that time (circa 1841) the first ever man-engine (which allowed miners to ride to surface, instead of climbing ladders) in Cornwall was installed at Tresavean. This engine, according to the late A. K. Hamilton Jenkin, was based upon a prize-winning model made for the Royal Cornwall Polytechnic Society by Michael Loam, the distinguished engineer. J. J. Pascoe insists in his *History of Adelaide*, however, that,

> The engineer of the mine (i.e. Loam) prepared a drawing, and Mr Martin was instructed to construct a model from it for submission to the gentleman who had to judge its merits. The contrivance was accepted, and . . . Mr Martin's model is treasured in the Polytechnic Hall in Falmouth.

James Martin, therefore, was displaying—even in those early years in Cornwall—the definite abilities of an accomplished craftsman and engineer. Nevertheless, for reasons that are not clear, he resigned his position at Tresavean and went to work in a mill at Ponsanooth. His deteriorating health may have had something to do with his abandoning his apprenticeship, however, for he suffered increasingly bad attacks of asthma, and indeed decided in 1847 to emigrate to South Australia in search of kinder climes. He arrived in Adelaide at the end of that year and, despite initial fears and misgivings, soon settled down in his new home. During 1848 he wrote to his friends in Stithians, describing the agricultural potential of the colony:

> . . . allow me to say, as the queen of Sheba did, the half was not told me. If ever you should come here I know you would like it . . . you will find it full of wheat, barley, and oats, vines and figs, almonds, peaches etc. etc., all bearing such a dark green colour, as you never saw in your life; a complete Paradise . . . . Behind the hills, there are tens of thousands of sheep and bullocks, grazing in the meadow land; with their hundreds of shepherds, giving us the best of beef and mutton for a penny to twopence per pound, and the flour as white as snow, at 12s per 112lbs; we shall have plenty of grapes and melons this year . . . . I very much regret not coming here before; remember me to my friends at Stythians. I thank God I never was better in my life.

James, perhaps, was thinking of his health when he noted the upturn in his fortunes in South Australia, but the economic implications of what he had to say would not have been lost upon his friends back in Cornwall. And it was in 1848 that James Martin purchased his shop in Gawler Town. He began by building bullock drays, much in demand from the farmers busily clearing the surrounding plains, and he recalled in later years that "For the first little while it was a terrible job to get along. Sometimes after paying my men only a portion of their wages, I had not 4d left to take a letter out of the P.O.". The continuing expansion of the agricultural frontier, however, led to an ever greater demand for agricultural implements—a demand Martin was able to meet by diversifying his production. He was one of the first to manufacture "stump-jump ploughs", a South Australia invention which proved to be of tremendous significance in clearing bush country, particularly the dreaded "mallee scrub" which covered many areas of the colony. The operation of the plough was simple enough; its ploughshare was so designed that it rose on striking a root or other concealed object and was then forced back into the ground by a hinged beam or draft chain. Martin recognised the importance of this innovation, and likewise was an early experimenter with double and multiple furrow ploughs.

By the 1860s, a time of mining expansion in South Australia, Martin's Foundry had grown considerably, and James Martin had acquired the plant, expertise and skilled labour to enable him to commence heavy mining engineering—recalling for him, perhaps, those early days at Tresavean. At first he produced Cornish boilers, but by the 1870s was turning out pump, whim and stamps engines. He also tried, but this time unsuccessfully, to establish iron smelting at Gawler, although the failure of that project in no way dampened his enthusiasm or damaged the long-term profitability of the Foundry. The rapid expansion of mining at Broken Hill in the 1880s and in Western Australia a decade later ensured that demand for his machinery would remain high, and in 1888 James Martin further diversified his production by securing an important contract for the construction of steam locomotives for the South Australian Railways.

James Martin himself became a prominent and respected local resident—Mayor of Gawler, Member of Parliament, and a leading figure in numerous local societies (including the Gawler Branch of the Cornish Association). At the time of his death in 1900, his works site covered 18 acres and the Foundry employed some 700 hands—making it Gawler's largest single employer—with orders for machinery coming from as far away as South Africa. "The Father of Gawler" was certainly a far cry from the sickly lad who had once mended cartwheels in Truro.

8. Gawler's tribute to James Martin, born in Stithians in 1821. Courtesy Jim Faull.

Almost inevitably, amongst the many craftsmen employed by James Martin was a number of Cornishmen. Indeed members of his own family joined him in the colony. His brother Felix arrived in Gawler in 1860 but soon afterwards died, James then accepting the guardianship of Felix's son—James Felix Martin—who in time became a partner in his uncle's business and was, according to Pascoe, ". . . one of the leading and most able businessmen of South Australia". Henry Rowe, another Cornishman, arrived in Gawler during 1862 and found employment in Martin's Foundry, working there as a wheelwright for some 10 years. And from the parish of Perranzabuloe came the talented May brothers. Frederick May was born in 1840 and arrived in the colony in 1858 to work as a mechanic at the Burra mine, moving from there to Yorke Peninsula where—at the age of 23—he became Chief Engineer of the Moonta Mines. In 1873 Frederick and his younger brother Alfred moved to Gawler as employees of James Martin, but in 1885 they established their own rival Foundry in the township, at first producing agricultural implements and later turning their hands—as James Martin had done—to supplying the demands of Australia's mining fields.

Between them, James Martin and the May Brothers dominated the Gawler industrial scene, but they did not entirely overshadow the efforts of other Cornishmen who became involved in the settlement of this important South Australian town. In fact, one of Gawler's earliest settlers was William Bassett, from Tredaule in the parish of Altarnun, who had arrived in the colony in 1840 in the "Java" and who in March 1845 acquired a section of the Gawler Special Survey, naming his suburb "Bassett Town". Another early arrival was Henry Mildren, from Helston, who set up a carpenter's shop in the township in 1847. And in 1852, John Harris—yet another Cornishman—purchased the "Gawler Stores", a local general store which Harris was able to expand into an important concern selling both general merchandise and agricultural implements.

In other areas of Gawler's commercial life it was also possible to spot the tell-tale traces of Cornishmen—John Allen opened his blacksmith's business in the township during 1852, Thomas Jones from Hayle set up a cobbler's shop—as did Philip Guy from Liskeard and James Short from Truro—and William

Wincey from Falmouth was a local timber merchant. Thomas Treleaven from Boscarne operated a carrying business in the district from 1879 until 1888, and Charles Courtis—born in Cornwall in 1844—was for many years foreman of the Gawler Corporation.

Gawler township, then, was not only an important settlement in its own right and a significant catalyst in the expansion of the South Australian agricultural frontier, but was also a major concentration of Cornish folk. It is especially significant that Cornish migrants were prominent in the establishment of the early rural settlements—such as Mount Barker, Willunga, and Gawler—and its equally telling that their contribution tended to be distinctive and in a way typically "Cornish"—as in the Willunga slate quarries or the Gawler engineering foundries—and that the Cornish folk tended to "stick together" through the medium of the Methodist chapels or social contact such as wrestling matches and Cornish Association meetings. It confirms that the Cornish impact in early South Australia was not confined to the efforts of the silver-lead and copper miners, and the many Cornish farm names that dot the Hills and Plains around Adelaide—"Millbrook", "Trevale", "Kersbrook", "Bowithick", "Carn Brea", "Carclew", "Trevalsa", "Roseworthy"—are as evocative and moving memorials to those Cornish pioneers as are the chimney stacks and engine-houses of the mining towns.

# CHAPTER 5

## Farming the Copper Kingdom—the Central Hill Country and Yorke Peninsula

The early establishment and rapid development of Gawler Town paved the way for the northward expansion of the agricultural frontier, but equally important in the late 1840s and 1850s were the large communities which grew up around the newly discovered copper mines at Kapunda and Burra. Later, in the 1860s and 1870s, the copper mining towns of Moonta, Wallaroo and Kadina were just as significant an impetus to the development of Yorke Peninsula as an agricultural district. The 1850s, of course, witnessed the huge jump in demand for wheat occasioned by the Gold Rush and the consequent rapid expansion of the Victorian population. But the South Australian population was also growing rapidly in the 1850s, the Government supporting an active immigration programme and the local economy gaining (after the initial traumas) from the high demand for its products from Victoria. South Australian wheat was then of an exceptionally high quality (one producer from Mount Barker won a gold medal at the Great Exhibition in London in 1851) and many local farmers were financially as successful—as a result of their wheat-growing efforts—as those who had actually done well digging for gold in Victoria.

The discovery of copper at Kapunda in 1843 and at Burra Burra in 1845 precipitated a large-scale Cornish migration to the colony, and around those two mines grew mining communities which exhibited all the signs of a distinct Cornish identity—the miners kept their traditional feasts and holidays, their mines were run according to the time-honoured tribute and tutwork system, Midsummer Bonfires were lit, as they were at home, the housewives baked their saffron cake and pasties, the men joined brass bands or entered the wrestling competitions, and of course the Methodist denominations—the "Bryanites", "Prims" and Wesleyans—built their ubiquitous chapels and held their tea-treats and Sunday School parades. Culturally and socially, therefore, the Cornish had made a major impact in the hitherto uninhabited Lower and Mid-North districts—the "Central Hill

66

Country" as geographer Michael Williams has called it—before the opening-up of the region for agriculture, an impact which would spill over inevitably into the surrounding communities as they emerged. It is in the environs of Kapunda and Burra Burra, then, that the distinction between "miner" and "non-miner", between mining expansion and agricultural expansion, becomes somewhat blurred, for they go hand-in-hand, and it is here that

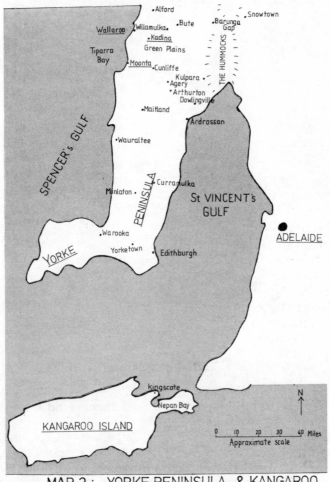

MAP 2 : YORKE PENINSULA & KANGAROO ISLAND

67

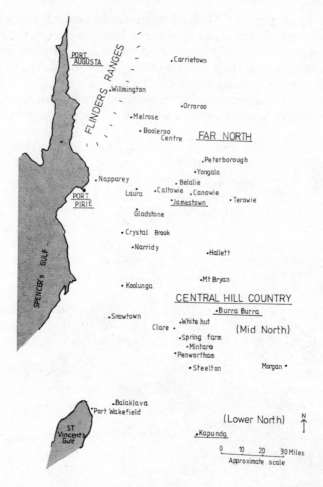

MAP 3: FAR NORTH & CENTRAL HILL COUNTRY

the link between mining and land settlement—and the Cornish role in both—is most noticeable.

The emergence of populous townships at both Kapunda and Burra Burra (there were 5,000 people at the Burra in 1850, then certainly the largest concentration of people in inland Australia) led inevitably to the development of all kinds of service industries in the district—general stores, bakers, butchers, wheelwrights, blacksmiths, builders, and so on. At the same time, the surrounding rural areas—until then considered inhospitable out-back regions unworthy of close settlement, at best pastoral land for sheep grazing—became the valuable hinterland of important economic centres, the mining towns. The mines also had a direct bearing on agricultural development, for settlers clearing their newly-acquired land were able to raise much-needed cash by selling waste timber to the mining companies as building materials and engine fuel, while any surplus hay would also be snapped up by the mine operators as feed for their whim-horses and bullock teams. Moreover, the miners themselves found the prospect of farming in the district increasingly attractive (many had been smallholders at home in Cornwall), and when they had saved enough money—usually through good fortune on the Victorian goldfields or as a result of a series of particularly successful tribute contracts—they purchased land in the area. The fact that the countryside surrounding both Kapunda and Burra Burra had neither the dense stringy-bark forest encountered in the Adelaide Hills nor the thick, impenetrable scrub found in other parts of the colony, but consisted instead of lightly-wooded savannah, made the region all the more attractive to prospective farmers.

Settlement in the wake of the Kapunda and Burra Burra mineral discoveries, then, took three forms: the tradesmen who arrived to establish the necessary service industries, the agriculturalists whose attentions were now focussed on the district, and the miners-turned-farmers who later acquired land in the area. Cornish immigrants, not surprisingly, were to be found in all three categories. At Kapunda many of the first to set up shop were Cornishmen, recognising no doubt that the high wages paid by the mine company would mean a high level of demand for their goods and services, a phenomenon some of them would have already seen at home in Cornwall on the occasion of the opening of a new mine. William Waters, for example, arrived in South Australia from Cornwall in 1840 at the age of 21, and by 1845 had opened his general store in the main street at Kapunda, living and working in the township for some 25 years. James Harris, who also arrived from Cornwall in 1840, ran a grocer's and draper's business in Kapunda, and James H. Pascoe found employment in various capacities in the township before selecting 536 acres of land at nearby Rose Hill. Of especial interest was Henry Binney Hawke, who arrived in the colony in 1857 at the age of 31. According to his biographer, Hawke had had a peculiarly eventful childhood, for he had been

> . . . orphaned at an early age. Whilst his younger sister was taken into the care of his mother's well-to-do relatives, young Hawke was adopted by Cornish smugglers who, in effect, became his uncles in thought and action . . . the impressionable Hawke must have entered the game (smuggling) with all his youthful zest, revelling in the escapades of his guardians, savouring the heady excitement of the chase and eluding his would-be captors.

Be that as it may, Hawke soon left his native Cornwall to go to London, where he earned 9d a week working in an engineering foundry. By 1857 he was in North Adelaide, again working in a foundry, and two years later he moved to Kapunda where he set up his own foundry business. The mine itself became an important source of orders for all kinds of engineering components, but Hawke also became noted for his high-quality cast-iron "lace-work" which graced many a Kapunda verandah, and by 1866—as a result of ". . . extensive improvements to the foundry . . ."—he was able to ". . . cater for farmers, millers . . . and machinists . . .". He also specialised in weighbridges, and in 1875 introduced his novel seed-sower. Hawke retired in 1883, selling his by now famous foundry to other businessmen in Kapunda.

At Burra Burra, many of the early artizans were also Cornish, and by 1855—as the *Royal South Australian Almanack and General Directory* illustrates—a fair number of the district's tradesmen, from the evidence of their surnames, hailed from Cornwall. William Bray was publican of the "Ancient Briton" at Kooringa (the principal Burra suburb) and Henry Nankervis was at the "Cross Roads Hotel". William Oliver was a local stonemason, J. Pearce was a sawyer, William Trembath a cobbler, Charles Rule a wheelwright, Robert Roach a baker, and so on. In later years Burra Burra retained its ability to attract Cornish artizans. Isaac Turner had arrived in the colony in the 1850s and worked at both Bowden and Kapunda before going to Kooringa to set up a brickmaking business, and his namesake—

John Turner—came out from Cornwall in 1872 to work at a grocer's shop at Burra Burra. In the same year George Sara arrived to establish a builder's business in partnership with John Dunstan, and six years later Ernest William Crewes from Truro found employment in Kooringa'a "Cornwall House" general store.

The Victorian Gold Rush proved an important stimulus to wheat-growers in the Central Hill Country, thus benefitting Cornish farmers who had already selected land in the area or were just arriving from Cornwall. Robert Wait gave up his employment as a Burra teamster to purchase land at nearby Pinkerton Plains, and William Escott—another Cornish teamster—selected 1087 acres near Burra Burra. John Fradd, also from Cornwall, bought 900 acres in the same area, while at nearby Riverton there was already a cluster of Cornish farmers— Richard Mitchell from Altarnun and his two sons at "Trenouth Farm", Samuel Jenkins at his 230 acre "Trewinna" property, and William Harris at his 200 acre "North Hill". On one such isolated property at Mount Bryan, to the north of Burra Burra, lived James Thomas who in a letter to his friends at Pencoys, near Redruth, wrote that "I often in my solitude live over again the happy hours that I spend amoung you in Cornwall". In that one short sentence we have a poignant insight into the loneliness endured by these early pioneers, living and working literally on the frontiers of European settlement. For all their apparent progress and success, these Cornishmen who first farmed the Central Hill Country of South Australia were faced with the daunting and often frightening task of taming what was then the "out-back".

The "miner-turned-farmer" phenomenon had manifested itself in quite early days—James Treloar, one Burra miner, had exchanged the pick for the plough as early as 1848—but most did not commence their farming activities until the 1850s, when the all-important Victorian Rush had both increased demand for wheat and provided many diggers with the means to purchase land. As before, the acreages taken on by these aspirant farmers would seem like vast estates to their friends and relatives back in Cornwall (though compared to later properties in the North they were in fact quite small), although the time and energy required to render the land fit for cultivation would also have horrified many a stay-at-home in the Old Country. John Curnow, for example, returned to Kapunda from the Rush and purchased a modest property. Unable to afford expensive clearing and ploughing machinery, however, he and his sons had the job of preparing their land, little by little, virtually by hand—their only implements being their spades. William Trevena, from Redruth, had little luck on the goldfields and returned to Kapunda with just enough money to purchase 300 acres but little else, though James Prior came back after only a few months with funds enough to purchase 617 acres at neighbouring Allendale. John Robins and his son William returned from Victoria wealthy enough to purchase a farm, a shop, and a flour mill to boot, and both Thomas Williams from St Austell and Thomas Badge—the Kapunda mine's engineer and blacksmith, respectively—came back with enough money to acquire land in the Central Hill Country.

At Burra Burra the story was much the same. James Sampson, from Goldsithney, was one of the first miners to farm in the district, and Henry Pinch from St Mabyn purchased his 784 acre farm "Pencarrow" after a particularly successful spell on the goldfields. William Pryor, born in St Austell in 1830, bought land at Baldina, and Alex Harris from Kenwyn was a "miner-turned-artizan"—a variation on the theme—having worked in the mines before becoming a local storekeeper. At Spring Farm, near the township of Clare, to the south of Burra Burra, there developed a veritable Cornish community, many of its members being former Burra miners and their families—William Mitchell, Edward Gray from Gwennap, Eliza Mitchell from Camborne, William Moyle, Thomas Bray from Hayle, Walter Treleaven, Thomas Thomas, John Roach, Joseph Prior, John and Mary Pearce, the Buzzacott family . . . .As noted in *The Cornish Miner in Australia*, these settlers became

> . . . close-knit, inter-married, carved out large farms with names such as "Trevenson" and "Treview", and moulded their social life through the medium of the local Wesleyan chapel. Samuel Bray and his wife Martha Glasson were both from Falmouth. Thomas Moyses lived at "Treview". His wife Mary was the sister of William Blight (from Pool) who was in turn married to Jane Bone

from St Just. Jane's brother James also lived in the district, and her son—William—married Mary Dunstone, a daughter of John Dunstone of "Trevenson". Thomas Ninnes (from Towednack) and John Chapman were other Cornish settlers. John married Amelia Teague (from North Hill), while another of the Chapmans, William, married Thomas Ninnes' daughter—Martha Maria. As time went on, these relationships became all the more complex, Spring Farm earning something of a reputation in the colony as a Cornish-Methodist stronghold.

It was Thomas Ninnes who in 1862 was responsible for opening the important Burra–Kadina track, when he and his colleagues from Clare blazed the trail through the Barunga Gap in the Hummocks range of hills, thus linking the two centres. Likewise, the Cornishmen moved on to other settlements in the Clare district. At Penwortham (which, despite its Cornish ring, was named after Penwortham Hall in Lancashire), to the south-east of Clare, Joseph Sleep purchased land after his return from the Rush, while at Mintaro William Sandow—from Chacewater—farmed his "Trelawney" property. At Hallett, to the north of Burra Burra, William Richards owned 1500 acres, while John Dunstan from Stithians possessed 1200 acres.

9. A team of "Sunshine" harvesters at Hallett, near Burra. Courtesy Ian Auhl.

73

The formation of a Clare Branch of the Cornish Association of South Australia in the 1890s provided a focal point for these widely scattered agriculturalists and their off-spring, but a more potent force—which had been excercised since the earliest days of settlement in the district—was of course that of Methodism. At first the settlers held services in their own homes, the local preachers riding across the country on horse-back to deliver their message to the outlying farms and hamlets such as White Hut, Seven Hills and Armagh. By 1853 the Wesleyans were ready to begin construction of their chapel at Spring Farm, the Brothers Bray, Moyses, Chapman and Treleaven undertaking the laborious work of carting the stone, sand and rubble for the building. The foundation stone was laid on 28 September 1853, the Adelaide *Observer* noting that

A more propitious day never increased the gladness of a joyous occasion, and the tent being left open on one side, the most picturesque scenery was presented to view, and rendered additionally attractive by the approach of numerous visitors from Kooringa, Mintaro, Penwortham, and Clare, and various surrounding localities, the growing prospects of a large harvest to come, and many actual proofs of a highly successful cultivation. About noon a large number of truly grateful guests partook of a Dinner which was most kindly and handsomely provided by Mr Samuel Bray ... Tables (were) surrounded by 100 guests, affording an "earnest" of future prosperity and peace in this 'Goshen of South Australia'. The tea meeting realised £10.00 ... It is said that the Chapel liabilities will be small, if they are not altogether extinguished by the crowning acts of liberality.

What is noticeable here, of course, is the link between the success of agriculture in the district, the "liberality" and enthusiasm of the local Methodists, and the consequent success of the chapel. John Rowe has suggested that there might indeed be a direct connection between religious "Revivals" in Cornish communities at home and abroad and upturns in economic progress. Certainly, the Cornish Methodists at Spring Farm and in the Clare district felt that they should offer thanks to God for their success, and their relative wealth enabled them to support the construction of a chapel and the financing of an active society.

An interesting story from one Spring Farm "Revival" has survived from those early days, recorded by the Rev. Stanley G.

Forth in his *Methodism in the Clare District*. According to the story, on the last day of the great "Revival" a penitent sinner ". . . who had sought peace every night at the Mission, went forward once more and knelt at the Rail, and prayed earnestly and with tears". At that moment another man, known in the district as a constant "back-slider", arrived in the chapel and also knelt at the Rail:

> The penitent looked up, saw whom it was, and at once turned to the back of the Chapel and seeing Father Moyses and William Blight together cried out in an agony of spirit 'Brother Moyses come and pray with me, I'll never find peace with Jimmy here, he never pays his debts'.

It might seem strange, in the light of the seriousness and commitment of the Cornish Methodist pioneers, that such a seemingly flippant anecdote should have survived. But it was in its way typical of the rather dry Cornish humour, in which the Cornish had the humility to laugh at themselves, and was of course very much in tune with the cartoons and Cousin Jack yarns of the late Oswald Pryor. As such, it was also indicative of the extent to which the Cornish way of life had come to permeate that part of the Central Hill Country. It was, as Forth noted, a district where ". . . Wesleyan hymns and prayers with a pronounced Cornish accent were to be heard echoing through the nearby scrub and stately gum trees". Spring Farm and Clare were the major Cornish concentrations among the agricultural communities, but the influence of Cornish Methodism ran to the most far-flung of the local centres of population—Phoebe Morcombe, from Kenwyn, was a Sunday School teacher at Auburn, Mary Jane Penrose was a Primitive Methodist at Morgan, and Charles Grey from Helston was a Bible Christian circuit steward and local preacher at Balaklava. Sampson Webb from Chacewater was a founding member of the Primitive Methodist chapel at Steelton, and at Mintaro there was an important knot of Cornish Bible Christians, the "Bryanites" there including the Trewrens, the Pauls, the Trelaggans from Gwennap, a Mrs Christopher from Sancreed, and William and Joseph Sandow from Chacewater.

Equally significant is the fact that, while in the 1850s the mighty Burra Burra was forced to suspend operations for several periods as a result of the labour shortages caused by the Victorian Gold Rush, there was nevertheless a significant Cornish movement to the land. In the 1860s, when the Burra began first to discern signs of its own decline, the Cornish agriculturalists were consolidating their newly-won properties, and in the 1870s—when the mine's fortunes began to decline alarmingly, culminating in closure in 1877—the farmers were experiencing a new wave of expansionist confidence, some even looking to pastures new along the Flinders' Ranges.

The 1850s had been a great era of agricultural expansion in South Australia. To some extent the momentum was carried on into the 1860s, but the mood of that decade was predominantly one of consolidation and reassessment, particularly so in the drought of 1864–65 when many pastoralists in remote areas lost large numbers of sheep and cattle. Demand from Victoria had also levelled-off by then, the heady days of the initial Rush having passed, and much of the agricultural land had become "wheat sick" as a result of over-concentration of production of that crop. There was also a shortage of good land for further expansion, many of the northern areas having been grabbed as "sheep run" pastoral properties and other districts consisting of seemingly impenetrable mallee scrub. In addition, many experts entertained strong doubts as to whether close settlement and agriculural pursuits could be supported in the relatively arid climes of the North.

However, South Australia was by no means at a stand-still in the 1860s, for the early years of that decade witnessed the discovery and rapid development of the Wallaroo and Moonta copper mines on northern Yorke Peninsula, an area soon to be known as "Australia's Little Cornwall" on account of the Cornish identity established there by the district's numerous Cornish immigrants. As at Burra Burra and Kapunda these new mines focussed attention on a hitherto uninhabited region and proved an important catalyst in the opening up of Yorke Peninsua for agricultural purposes. In the first place, the emergence of Wallaroo, Moonta and Kadina as large centres of population led to the establishment of all kinds of service industries and, as in the Central Hill Country, the Peninsula's rural expanses were opened up by farmers whose attentions were now drawn to the district and, in time, by miners-turned-farmers from "Little Cornwall" itself.

Before the Wallaroo and Moonta discoveries, there had been a sprinkling of settlers on Yorke Peninsula—pastoralists who had leased large tracts of land which they did not improve but used merely for the grazing of their sheep and other stock. Walter Watson Hughes, the Scottish sea-captain from Pittemweem in the county of Fife upon whose property the Wallaroo mines were first discovered, was one such pastoralist. Another was John Bowden, the Cornishman from Kersbrook in the Adelaide Hills, who acquired a sheep run on the Peninsula as early as 1847, in 1851 taking out a 14 year lease on 107 square miles in the region of what were later to be Yorketown and Edithburgh. Although described by the modern local historian Ern Carmichael as ". . . a very industrious Cornishman . . .", Bowden's reputation at the time was hardly enviable. In 1848 Inspector Tolmer—one of early Adelaide's great "characters"—was in pursuit of a band of dangerous, escaped Tasmanian convicts who were thought to be on the loose on Yorke Peninsula. Eventually, their camp was discovered on Bowden's run, but when Tolmer asked him to lead him to the spot so that the arrests could be made, Bowden ". . . demurred, making several paltry excuses . . .". According to the worthy Inspector's account of the story, Bowden was persuaded to afford his assistance only after Tolmer had been ". . . compelled to impress him in the Queen's name . . .".

In 1853 John Bowden was again the subject of Adelaide gossip when he was sued successfully for £960 damages in the South Austraian Supreme Court over a breach of agreement concerning the sale of some 4,000 of his sheep. At the same time, his sons left him to try their luck in Victoria, and poor Bowden—by now thoroughly disillusioned—abandoned the run to return to his wife and homestead at Kersbrook. It is easy, perhaps, to condemn Bowden for his foolishness, but in a way his experiences point to the difficulties, dangers, loneliness and subsequent insecurities with which early pastoralists in remote areas had to contend.

Amongst the other early pastoralists on Yorke Peninsula was Dick Lander, a Cornishman and nephew of the celebrated Richard Lander of Nigeria, who grazed 26,000 sheep on the

Peninsula from 1861 until 1866. There was also Stephen Goldsworthy, who had arrived from Cornwall in 1846 and had acquired land at Black Point, on Yorke Peninsula, in 1855. His five sons later purchased properties in the area, one of them— William Higgs Goldsworthy of Curramulka—becoming one of the most important farmers on mid-Yorke Peninsula.

By the early 1860s, of course, the townships of Moonta, Wallaroo and Kadina were already established, the character of the district being overwhelmingly Cornish, and in the wake of the miners came the inevitable artizans and commercialists. As at Kapunda and Burra Burra, they included numerous Cornishmen. At Moonta, for example, one of the earliest settlers was a certain Joseph Williams. He was born in Wendron in 1837 and arrived in the colony in 1848, moving to Moonta in 1861 to establish a butcher's business as soon as the mines were discovered. He lived in the township until his death in 1911. William Chappell, from Illogan, was another early arrival, setting up his cobbler's shop in George Street, Moonta, in 1864. There was also James Trezona,

10. William Chappell's cobbler's shop, George Street, Moonta, circa 1880. Chappell came from Illogan and set up his business in Moonta in 1864. Courtesy South Australian Archives.

a local storekeeper, and John Phillips who worked in Moonta as a mason and a hairdresser—". . . the two trades of which he was master . . .", to quote one contemporary report!

Richard Lawry from St Ives ran a general store in Moonta township, Edward Pollard from Newlyn built the first lime kiln at East Moonta, and William Abrahams managed the "Miners' Arms Hotel". Ephraim Major, born in St Ives in 1842, was a coach-builder, wheelwright and blacksmith in Moonta for many years, while James Jewell, born at Troon in October 1840, was a local plumber and iron merchant. John Tippett Harris from Truro ran the local bakery, and in 1870 James Tiddy from St Mawes opened his draper's store in the township. Sampson James from St Ives and William Cowling from Calstock were both cobblers, John Beaglehole from Helston was a mason, John Symons from Chacewater was an auctioneer, and Michael Whitburn from Praze-an-Beeble was an agent for the local "Farmers' Co-oprative Union".

Moonta's Cornishmen, then, were by no means all miners. And by observing just how quickly and how comprehensively the Cornish settled into all these other occupations, we can imagine how truly "Cornish" was the ambience of old Moonta, and how deservedly apt was the sobriquet "Australia's Little Cornwall". There can have been few settlements outside Cornwall itself which, culturally and in terms of social composition, were as overwhelmingly Cornish as Moonta in the nineteenth century. Northern Yorke Peninsula's other principal townships, Kadina and Wallaroo, shared too in Moonta's Cornish identity, and in those settlements there was also more than a sprinkling of Cornish colonists. The *Adelaide Almanack Town and Country Directory* for 1865 showed that even at that early date Cornish artizans were well-entrenched in Wallaroo: Henry Bawden and George Brock were both carpenters, William Madden was a mason, William Bray and Erasmus Paull were carters, John Oates was a teamster, and Mark Hocking, William Jewell and William Trelease were all employed in the smelting works erected at Wallaroo for the purpose of smelting copper ore from the local mines. William Phillips, from Gwennap, was another smelter—in the 1870s he became Mayor of Wallaroo.

Of particular importance was William Henry May. He was a

member of the celebrated and talented May family from Perranzabuloe and, like his brothers Frederick and Albert (who opened a foundry at Gawler), he had arrived in the colony to work as an engineer at the Burra Burra mine but had later moved to Yorke Peninsula. In 1875 he joined forces with another Cornishman, a certain Stephen Tonkin, to open an engineering foundry in Wallaroo township. Tonkin left the partnership in 1881, leaving William in sole command of the increasingly successful and ultimately renowned establishment which gave South Australian agriculturalists such inventions as the "Little Marvel" harvester and the "Twin Skim" plough.

11. The foundry opened by William Henry May, from Perranzabuloe, at Wallaroo in 1875. Courtesy South Australian Archives.

At Kadina there was any number of Cornish tradesmen—John Liddicoat, carpenter, James Martin, butcher, Samuel Mutton, carter, R. V. Rodda, photographer, Anthony Sando, bootmaker, and so on. The butcher, James Martin, was born at Plain Cross in the parish of Perranarworthal in 1835, emigrating to South Australia in 1853 onboard the "Thetis". He settled at first at the Burra, but in April 1861 moved to the newly-established township of Kadina where he became one of its first traders by opening—on 12 May—his butcher's business. In later years he purchased a 2,000 acre farm in the district, and was for a time Mayor of Kadina as well as an active and respected member of such local instituions as the "Kadina Horticultural and Floral Society". Another well-known Kadina identity was Henry Nankervis, who built and ran the "Kadina Hotel" from 1861 until 1873, and at the "Wombat Hotel" was Daniel Dunn—a former miner from St Austell who had arrived in the colony in 1865 and had decided to try his hand as a hotelier in 1874. The Rosewarne family, from Phillack, had arrived in South Australia in 1857 and moved to the Kadina district in 1861, opening a blacksmith's and wheelwright's business there in 1882.

The development of farming on Yorke Peninsula did not immediately follow the opening of the local copper mines, partly because of the arid and inhospitable nature of the surrounding countryside—it consisted mainly of salt-bush and mallee scrub—but also due to the fact that the early 1860s witnessed a slowing of the pace of rural expansion in South Australia generally. The needs of the mines and mining communities were, of course, a stimulus to agricultural development, and in 1863—four years after the discovery of the Wallaroo Mines—the first Hundreds on northern Yorke Peninsula were proclaimed. But it was not until May 1866, when 300 acres of wheat were sown at Greens Plains, near Kadina, that the district began cereal production. In July of that year a survey of non-mining land was made in the districts of Wallaroo, Tipara, Kulpara, and Port Arthur, and, with the passing of the all-important Strangway's Act in 1868, the northern part of the Peninsula became available to farmers.

Strangway's Act was the result of concern in Government circles in Adelaide about the colony's relative agricultural decline and the fear that South Australia's rural population was about to forsake the colony in favour of Victoria (there was little evidence to support this fear, but the traumatic effects of the early Victorian Gold Rush—when so many had left for the neighbouring colony—was still very much in people's minds). In 1867 the Government made three million acres of frontier mallee land available for selection by farmers, and then presented Strangway's Bill which very shortly became law. Under the terms of the act, land could for the first time be bought on credit over four years, with an interest rate of five per cent per annum, purchasers being required to settle on their land and to improve it to the value of 12s 6d per acre. This, of course, discouraged the practice of "absentee landlordism", ensured that the land opened up for cultivation would indeed be improved, and gave the "small man" of limited means the ability to acquire farming land. This latter point was not lost on the Peninsula miners, many of whom—like their compatriots at Kapunda and Burra Burra—wished to change from mining to farming, to be at last their own "bosses".

In the wake of Strangway's Act, Yorke Peninsula was opened up quickly for agricultural purposes. Throughout the early 1870s new farming communities sprang up, and as they emerged so new ports were built along the Peninsula's coastline to facilitate the export of wheat and the import of agricultural materials and implements. Geography was kind to the Yorke Peninsula settlers,

12. Grain ships alongside at Wallaroo. Port Wallaroo was an important departure point for the agricultural produce of Yorke Peninsula. Courtesy South Australian Archives.

for nowhere was far from the sea, sea-traffic being by far the most efficient mode of transport in the colony at that time—but only if one lived near the coast, of course!

John Nankivell, who had arrived in South Australia from Cornwall in 1848, was reputed to be amongst the first to begin farming on northern Yorke Peninsula. And the first of the district's miners-turned-farmers was possibly John Phillips, born at Wendron in 1815, who purchased land at Greens Plains as soon as it became available. Others, like Joseph Rodda from Kadina, were quick to follow his example, and in July 1870 the Adelaide *Observer* could note with obvious pride in the achievement that ". . . Green's Plains is gradually being occupied for agricultural purposes . . . . Farmers are struggling manfully to supplant mallee scrub with cornfields".

In 1872 Strangway's Act was improved and up-dated, and this combined with a series of excellent harvests in the early 1870s and various attendant improvements in agricultural technology to increase the clamour for more land to be made available and for land laws to be further liberalised. In May 1873 an editorial in the *Yorke's Peninsula Advertiser* called for greater agricultural expansion in the district. Twelve months later a petition from Peninsula miners calling on the colonial Government to open up land in the Hundreds of Kadina, Kulpara, Wallaroo and Cameron was presented to the Parliament in Adelaide. They emphasised, quite rightly of course, that many of them had had some farming experience at home in Cornwall and were therefore well-placed to make the move from mining to farming. On the whole, Governments in the 1870s needed little prompting to get on with the business of frontier expansion, the Ministries of the Cornishman James Penn Boucaut being especially associated with this renewed enthusiasm for agricultural growth.

By August 1875 Bawden's agricultural foundry at Kadina was busily producing implements for local farmers, and more and more land on the Peninsula was opened up for farming purposes. In June 1876 the *Yorke's Peninsula Advertiser* could note that ". . . land in the vicinity is being taken up . . . and cultivation is transforming that which was a desert and scrubby waste . . .". A drought in the summer of 1876–77 drove some off the land and deterred others from purchasing property, but nevertheless it was recorded with some satisfaction in January 1878 that one-third of the entire area of Yorke Peninsula was now used for farming and grazing, while the region's wheat output amounted to one million bushels, worth some £250,000.

Needless to say, a very great many of these farmers responsible for the cultivation of Yorke Peninsula were Cornishmen, and in the north of the region the Cornish were fairly clearly in the majority. Some had worked as small farmers or agricultural labourers at home in Cornwall and had emigrated to South Australia in the hope of being able to buy land. Such was the case of James Bettess from Launceston who arrived in South Australia in March 1877 and eventually selected land at Bute, and of Joseph and Harriett Colliver from Baldhu who had arrived in the colony in 1855 and later purchased property at Arthurton, giving their farm the touchingly optimistic name "Sunny Hill".

Most of the Cornish farmers on northern Yorke Peninsula were, as one would expect, former miners. John Thomas from Penzance, for example, had been a Burra miner before dabbling in other occupations and finally selecting land at Bute. In 1873 William Andrew, a miner from Breage, purchased 419 acres near Wallaroo Mines, while William Jenkin from Redruth selected land at Greens Plains, and James Trengove from Caradon Town farmed at Barunga and later at Bute. John Liddicoat, another Cornishman, took a modest 39 acres in the district in 1875, and in the following year Paul Roach—from Ludgvan—purchased 389 acres near Kadina with the £450 he had saved from several tribute "sturts" (strikes of rich ground in the mines). Thomas Rodda took land in the vicinity at the same time, while in 1877 Richard Stephens (from Trevarren in the parish of St Columb) took 340 acres at Kulpara. John King, born in Cornwall in 1842, bought 424 acres at Wallaroo in 1877, and Thomas and Richard Chappell—from Polgooth—selected land at Alford in the Hundred of Tickera. Richard Borlace went into partnership with a Mr Prowse to farm at Wallaroo, while David Edyvean acquired 1500 acres near Kadina in 1878. Elsewhere in the district the Cornish were equally thick on the ground; miners-turned-farmers who had participated in the great expansion of the 1870s: Richard Ford from Gwennap, John Thomas from St Ives, James Quintrell from Porthleven, William Rowe Manuel from Lanner,

13. An eighteen-bullock team at work on Cliff Rodda's farm, near Kadina. Courtesy South Australian Archives.

Reuben Glanville Cock from Liskeard, Paul Barbary from St Austell, Andrew Daddow, William Trethowan, Alfred Tresize, and many, many more.

But despite their ardour and enthusiasm, the process of winning the land was never easy. One contemporary account recalled how Benjamin Rose "With not a few others from Moonta Mines . . . tackled the mallee country for which Yorke Peninsula was famous . . . (a task) which might have been described as penal servitude for life". Similarly, Charles Wesley Bowden remembered that,

> In the year 1875, my parents selected Section 319 in Agery, Hundred of Tiparra, and proceeded to clear the block and erect a home. Until the first two rooms of wattle and daub (typical of miners' homes) were completed, they travelled from Moonta Mines on Hamley Hill daily by horse and cart—no mean feat.

Bushfires were a constant threat in the summer months, of

course, and in 1878 Richard Stephens lost his entire 340 acres at Kulpara when it was struck by fire. And after a decade of feverish expansion in the 1870s came the drought of 1881 to 1891 (the worst years were 1881, 1885, 1888 and 1891) and the economic downturn of the 1880s and 1890s. The introduction of super-phosphate saved many a Peninsula farmer, but numerous others shared the fate of Harry Hooper's parents. Harry wrote that in the early 1880s,

> When we went on the land towards Cunliffe . . . Father had a single furrow plough and an old spring dray patched up with "cocky" vine on the shafts, spokes etc. At this time wheat was one and sixpence a bushel and my parents took eggs to Moonta for which the stores allowed them twopence a dozen . . . . Father sold out for £1 2s od per acre; a few years later, after the introduction of superphosphate, the same land was worth £12 to £15 an acre.

A similar tale of woe was that of Elisha Mayne. He had arrived in the colony circa 1855 and, although he was sending money back to Cornwall to support both his mother and mother-in-law, he had managed to save the extremely large sum of £700 by 1875. He decided, therefore, to purchase 200 acres of land on the Kadina–Moonta road, about mid-way between the two towns. Although it only cost him £1 per acre to buy, he had to employ casual labour to clear the dense scrub, the final cost of purchase and clearance being nearer £4 per acre—or £800. Already in debt, he had yet to purchase machinery and supplies, and it was a wonder that he struggled on as he did until January 1877 when, succumbing to drought and debt, he was forced to sell his land and abandon farming.

Throughout the 1880s other Cornish settlers on Yorke Peninsula were forced to make the same decision. In January 1882 it was said that Isaac Polkinghorne ". . . intends leaving the district . . ." (he was offering 440 acres of cleared land for sale), while in October 1883 Richard Scoble was giving up his 242 acres at Greens Plains, and in September 1884 W. Chenoweth was selling his farm to go to Victoria. Some decided to move on to New South Wales or New Zealand, others wanted to return to Cornwall, and still others—like William Ellis, from Penzance—had little alternative but to go back to mining. Smallholders especially were hard hit, and many left the land—George Rule,

86

B. G. Axford, William Veal, Paul Daniels, James Wearne, Ralph Williams, J. J. Langdon, and countless more. The only ones who benefitted from the difficult days of the 1890s were those who managed to last out, acquiring the properties of their less fortunate neighbours at low prices, thus achieving various economies of scale and also gaining from later improvements in agricultural machinery and technology. Those who did survive were lucky for, with the return of brighter economic conditions and wetter winters, Yorke Peninsula became established in the early years of this century as a principal wheat-growing district.

14. A billy-goat cart full of "motts" (a Cornish-South Australian word for mallee roots, stumps and sticks) on the Yorke Peninsula settlement. Courtesy South Australian Archives.

In a manner reminiscent of the experience in the Central Hill Country, the movement outwards from the Peninsula mining towns to the surrounding countryside in the late 1860s and 1870s was matched by an accompanying Cornish social and cultural impact in the new agricultural communities. Cornish wrestlers travelled from outlying farms to Moonta or Kadina to participate in competitions, local literary and choral societies organised Cornish Carol concerts and dialect recitations, and—most importantly—the Methodist denominations constructed new chapels in the rural areas. J. V. Morgan has noted in his *Colonial Methodism in South Australia* that "Methodism was pioneered at Maitland from Wallaroo, Moonta and Kadina", the "Word" being brought to Maitland—and many other similar Peninsula townships—by Missionaries from "Little Cornwall" and by the miners-turned-farmers who had settled in the district. At the laying of the foundation stone at the Maitland Wesleyan chapel in August 1875, for example, Captain T. Tregoweth (a Cornish mine manager) was in attendance and the Rev. Thomas Rowe (a Cornish minister) officiated.

And when Reuben Gill—the Peninsula's famous Bible Christian local preacher, trade union activist and Temperance advocate, known to his admirers as "The Billy Bray of South Australia"—embarked upon a five week lecturing tour of central and southern Yorke Peninsula in 1883 he found that the Methodist and Temperance bodies had already prepared the ground-work well. At Yorketown, Gill spoke on "The Delusion of Strong Drink", but only one listener came forward to sign the "pledge"—all the rest, or so the contemporary newspaper report would have us believe, were teetotallers already. At Warooka the experience was the same, and at Minlaton—although some had "fallen"—he found a strong Rechabite tent, a juvenile Rechabite tent, and a "huge" Band of Hope—some children walking five to seven miles through the bush to attend the meetings. Maitland was also strong, while "Wauraltee holds her own . . . Ardrossan has started a band of hope. Dowlingville is firm to a man, to a boy, to a girl . . .".

At Kulpara, one of the northern Yorke Peninsula settlements founded by former miners, John Prisk—another of Moonta's well-known Bible Christian and trade union activists—actually designed the local chapel and supervised its construction. At Willamulka, near Bute, a certain H. Rodda was responsible for the erection of the diminutive Bible Christian chapel in 1884, with the Bettess family from Launceston and the Trengoves from Caradon Town becoming involved in the society at about the same time. James Trengrove was a Bible Christian preacher in the district for 33 years, and his fifth son, Arthur, was ordained as a minister.

On Yorke Peninsula, then, as in the Central Hill Country, the Cornish settlers spread rapidly to new areas as they were opened for cultivation, taking their Cornish ways and their Cornish Methodism with them. In so doing they established an enduring Cornish impact and ensured that families of Cornish descent would remain in the area long after the demise of the copper mines. Kapunda and Burra Burra closed in 1876 and 1877, and Moonta and Wallaroo were abandoned in 1923, but even today—flicking through a local telephone directory and glancing for a moment at the list of names—one might be forgiven for imagining that one was in Cornwall.

# CHAPTER 6

## Rain Follows the Plough—or does it?

South Australia's neighbours had been content to build their rural activities upon the pastoral industry, the grazing of huge flocks of sheep and cattle over vast tracts of largely unimproved outback country, allowing South Australia to become the continent's "granary". However, despite the concern for closer settlement and the expansion of the wheat frontier, South Australia also developed her own pastoral industry—in many areas the pastoralists preceding, almost pointing the way for, the later agriculturalists. This was certainly the case, as we have seen, on Yorke Peninsula, but it was also true for the remote areas beyond the Central Hill Country and into the southern Flinders' Ranges—the colony's so-called "Far North".

Large quantities of stock were brought overland from the eastern colonies during the 1840s, the pastoral pioneers continually pressing into more and more remote country—into the south-east, onto Eyre Peninsula, and into the Far North. As a measure of this expansion, by 1856 Wooltana sheep station had been established 200 miles north-east of Port Augusta. Port Augusta had been surveyed in 1854 and, with its important position at the head of Spencer's Gulf, became a vital outlet and supply centre for, in turn, the region's pastoral, mining, and agricultural industries.

In good times, pastoral pursuits were remarkably lucrative, but the life of the outback pastoralist was often dangerous and always lonely. The existence of the outback shepherd was especially unenviable, faced as he was by unrelieved solitude amid the awesome expanses of the interior. To those brought up in the Cornish countryside, with its pattern of patchwork fields and little churchtowns, the impact of life on the outback properties could be immense, sometimes desperately so. The *South Australia Register*, for example, noted the suicide in 1862 of poor James Dunstan, ". . . a native of Cornwall . . .", an outback shepherd who hanged himself in his little wooden hut in the middle of nowhere. Droughts, too, could have a devastating effect, the first really serious drought to be experienced being that of 1864–65. Some 17,000 square miles of land along the Flinders' Ranges were drought-stricken, huge flocks of sheep and herds of cattle perishing as their saltbush pastures turned to desert, and amongst those pastoralists most sorely hit was Hillary Boucaut, from Saltash.

Hillary Boucaut had arrived in South Australia from Cornwall in 1846 with his parents, later taking up pastoral properties in the Far North and the south east. The drought of 1864–65 left him virtually ruined (he sold out to another Cornishman, one John Rounsevell), though his brother James Penn Boucaut did what he could for Hillary and the other stricken pastoralists by bringing their troubles to the attention of the Adelaide Parliament and winning various relief measures. This experience no doubt gave James the interest in the northern frontier which he was to exhibit again in the 1870s, but in the mid-1860s the lessons learnt from the drought seemed to be largely cautionary.

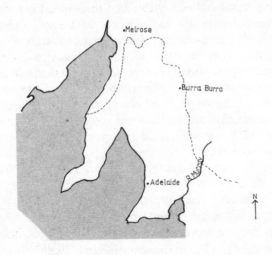

## MAP 4 : GOYDER'S LINE OF RAINFALL

In 1865 George Goyder, the Surveyer General, drew a line on the map of South Australia to mark the southern limit of the drought or, in the words of the Parliamentary Paper of the time, to act as ". . . the line of demarcation between that portion of the country where the rainfall has extended, and that where the drought prevails". At the time it was drawn, "Goyder's Line" (as it was thereafter known) was not intended necessarily as a boundary between land that could be cultivated successfully and that which could not. But, perhaps inevitably, that quickly became the popular interpretation. The line itself, on the map, began on the west coast of Yorke Peninsula, some way south of Moonta, and swept inland, by-passing the mining towns and sweeping northwards. It continued north, a considerable distance from the coast, until it reached Melrose when it looped southwards, then sweeping down the east side of the Mount Lofty Ranges (Burra lay just inside the line) before crossing the Murray and disappearing into the south east.

At first "Goyder's Line" appeared as something of a daunting frontier, a boundary between life and death, success and failure, a frontier to be approached with trepidation and misgivings. However, potential agriculturalists soon began to reason that, if the line did mark the boundary between cultivatable and non-cultivatable land, then surely it was reasonable to open up for agricultural purposes those as yet unsurveyed districts lying inside the line. Strangways Act in 1869 facilitated the movement of farmers into those areas, and those who did move in were mostly successful. Encouraged by this success, the Government began to plan new townships in the northern districts—more than 100 were surveyed in the decade up to 1879, putting new names such as Booleroo Centre, Gladstone, Crystal Brook and Jamestown onto the map of rural South Australia.

Boucaut's railways, part of his grand expansionist scheme introduced in 1875, went inland from Port Augusta, Port Pirie and Port Wakefield, penetrating the newly-developed areas. The weather, too, seemed to be on the settlers' side, the good seasons of the early 1870s appearing to confirm this wisdom of the agricultural expansion. Clearing the land, of course, was—as elsewhere—a time-consuming and costly business, but new techniques were constantly developed. The stump-jump plough eased the problem of ploughing recently cleared land, and the actual process of clearance was helped by the emergence of the art of "mullenizing" whereby a heavy roller was used to knock down the mallee scrub trees, the scrub then being allowed to dry out before being burnt. A crop of wheat was then grown, and after it was harvested the stubble was burnt off, the new mallee shoots and any remaining old roots being destroyed.

The expansion of the wheat frontier in the 1870s was reminiscent of the great expansion of the 1850s, and farmers and politicians alike were keen to see the frontier pressed on, beyond "Goyder's Line". The line was approached, crossed, and passed—all seemingly without problem—the Government sanctioning the move in 1874, and the excellent harvests of 1877 to 1879 appeared to underline the wisdom of this expansion. People, it seems, really did believe the old adage that "rain follows the plough", even the better-educated rationalising this superstition by arguing that cultivation—in particular the planting of trees—increased rainfall (on the strength of this argument, 60,000 trees were planted near Jamestown in eight years).

Mining also served as an impetus to the development of the Far North, although it was much less an influence that in the Central Hill Country or on Yorke Peninsula. Nevertheless, the success of the northern regional centre of Hawker was aided by the existence of several copper mines in the locality (opened up in the 1860s in the wake of the spectacular Moonta and Wallaroo finds) such as the Arkaba Creek, the Wirrawilka, and the Appeanilla. At Blinman was the important Wheal Blinman mine, together with other workings owned by the Yudnamutana Copper Co, and in the Carrieton-Mattawarangala stretch of the Flinders' Ranges was a number of important mines, most notably the Prince Alfred. The development of these mines in the 1860s and 1870s (though few survived through to the 1890s or beyond) had the additional effect of drawing Cornish miners to the Far North, and the closure of the Kapunda and Burra Burra mines in the late 1870s created a pool of unemployed Cornishmen looking for work—in new mines or on new farms. A number, indeed, found lucrative employment as well-sinkers on new agricultural properties in the Far North, the Burra Burra mine noting in 1876 that men were leaving its employ for that purpose.

93

The Cornish, as usual, played their part in this renewed expansion of the South Australian agricultural frontier. The township of Port Pirie was laid-out in 1872 as a maritime outlet for the agricultural produce of the northern districts and by 1873 boasted a population of 160. William Henry Skewes, from Redruth, opened a chemist's shop in the township in 1877, and in the same year Thomas Bowden arrived from Portleven. In Cornwall he had worked in his father's boatbuilding business, and so it was not surprising that Bowden should open his own boatbuilder's firm in Port Pirie, responding to the port's ever-increasing demand for maritime craft.

William Henry Moyle, born in Redruth in 1836, also arrived in Port Pirie in 1877, after a rather mobile career in both South Australia and North America which had seen him erecting Cornish engines on the Lake Superior mines at the age of 22 but only a year later working at Kapunda. At Port Pirie he was employed as a flour mill engineer, processing the grain from the surrounding wheat districts, but later purchasing an aerated water factory—"Moyle's Lemonade" becoming almost a household name in the thirsty climes of rural South Australia! Other Port Pirie notables included Richard and Harry Sampson, from Liskeard, who were butchers and shipping agents in the town, and Thomas Major—another Cornishman who, after a chequered existence on the Victorian goldfields, in New Zealand, and at Moonta, became a local hotelier and ultimately Mayor of Port Pirie.

In the wake of Port Pirie's development came the rush to farm the Far North. At Port Augusta James Bryant, a Cornishman, made his money as a contracter serving the rapidly expanding wheat frontier, while other Cousin Jacks participated in this northerly thrust. Some had come from Yorke Peninsula, others from Kapunda and Burra Burra, a number from Gawler or the other centres of population, and still others from the Central Hill Country where, to quote one local historian, "many of the Cornishmen, with little hope of expansion on small farms around Penwortham, sold out and headed north". In 1875 Ludgvan-born James Thomas was one of the first settlers in the Hundred of Narridy, to the south east of Port Pirie. He was a former Burra miner, but had been in the extreme far North since 1857 on his

Umberatana Station property. John Nunan, another Cornishman, moved from Gawler to take up land in the Hundreds adjoining Port Pirie, and in 1871 William Pengilly became one of the earliest farmers at Koolunga. At nearby Laura, there were the Bryants from Hayle and Joseph Sibley, a Cornishman who had moved up from Strathalbyn in 1872. Another Cousin Jack, Paul Martin, ran the general store at Caltowie—one of the newly laid-out townships—until 1886.

15. A typical limestone-constructed homestead in the Far North of South Australia. Courtesy Jim Faull.

Belalie was one of the new northern districts opened up after Strangway's Act and the crossing of "Goyder's Line". During the 1870s Edward Dunstan, from Wendron, purchased 240 acres of virgin bush land in the district. He was a man of considerable experience, having mined at Kapunda, Yudnamutana, Blinman and in Victoria, Queensland and New Zealand, before deciding to turn his hand to farming. Nevertheless, as Nancy Robinson explains in her history of the sourthern Flinder's Ranges, the decision to farm was a momentous and far-reaching one. Dunstan himself described the problems of selecting land:

Having decided to take up land, Mr William Symons, my brother-in-law, and I rode up from Kapunda to look over the country. We travelled light, with a blanket strapped to the saddle. The first night we camped at a spot near what is now Bundaleer North. We rode over the country (at Belalie) examining it carefully, camped a night at Mount Lock, then at Nanowie . . . . We thought that the Northern end of Belalie was the best land but had the serious disadvantage of not having water available. Finally we selected our land near the surveyed township of Jamestown for the convenience of obtaining water supply and education of our children. I took section 89 . . . and Mr Symons selected a block just across the Caltowie road.

Dunstan continued,

Having become the owner of a piece of virgin unfenced land; our next problem was to get a piece ploughed up to be sown so that we would have seed for the next season. I managed to get six acres ploughed, put in a bag of wheat and reaped ten in return, which seemed very good. Then there was fencing to be done. There was no timber nearer than Wirrabarra, 25 miles distant. Often I worked part of the day on the farm then put the horses in and went as ar as the Rocky River that night, camped there, drove into the Forest next morning, loaded up with posts and out to the Rocky again that afternoon, rested and fed the horses and travelled during the night reaching home perhaps at daylight.

Such were the rigours of pioneering life in colonial South Australia, and Edward Dunstan's experiences would have been typical of countless others on the wheat frontier in the 1870s. Life for the tradesmen in the new townships was marginally less hard than that of the farmers (the worry of making a new business pay its way was at least less exhausting physically than clearing a new farm). Jamestown, with its enormously wide streets, solid, stone-built shops and dwellings, and its rather sombre atmosphere, was one of the new Government townships and—as Edward Dunstan intimated—an important focal point for settlers in the surrounding countryside. It grew rapidly in the 1870s to meet the demands of the local agriculturalists, Francis Opie—born in Stithians in 1846—moving to Jamestown from Adelaide in 1876 to open a small foundry which specialised, not surprisingly, in the manufacture of agricultural implements.

Thomas Trevena arrived in the township from Kapunda with his wife, Amelia Menhennet, to open a store, while Helston-born Edward Wills travelled down from Port Augusta for the same purpose. William Roberts, born in St Austell in 1834, opened a greengrocer's shop in Jamestown, while in 1879 Thomas Axford from Chacewater purchased the general-store in the township's main street. William Treleaven, originally from Nanstallon, moved his carrying business from Adelaide to Jamestown to be able to tap the lucrative demand of the northern frontier, living and working in the town for more than 30 years.

16. Jamestown, circa 1876. Courtesy South Australian Archives.

Terowie, less than 20 miles to the north east of Jamestown, was another of the new townships. Thomas Hosking and his wife Margaret (born in Penzance in 1821) opened the first shop in Terowie, while James Roach left his farm at White Hut, near Clare, to purchase new property near Terowie township in 1875. And in the neighbouring district of Yongala there was, as Gladys Ward has shown, a number of ". . . agriculturalists from the Burra . . ."—local Cornish settlers including James Cook and his wife Ann Tresise, Richard Tyack Glasson, John Jennings, and Charles Thomas.

The districts of Booleroo, Melrose, and Orroroo could also boast sizeable Cornish contingents—in some ways reminiscent of the Spring Farm concentration in the Central Hill Country, but on a rather more far-flung scale. John Sanders had arrived in

South Australia in the "Omega" in 1851, and worked as a miner at both Burra Burra and Moonta before becoming one of the first settlers at Booleroo when he took up sections in the district in December 1875. Henry Bastian and his wife Ann Northey (from Truro) lived at Kapunda, where Henry worked at the mine, before selecting land at Booleroo. Their son Alfred, born in Cornwall in 1839, farmed an adjoining property, while in the same district were the farms of William Besanko Martin, Samuel Arthur, and William Polglase. There was also John Dunstan, another Kapunda miner, who owned 900 acres at Booleroo, and Henry Waters from Penzance who had been at both Kapunda and Kadina before selecting section 118 in the Hundred of Booleroo in 1877. Some years later William Nottle from Probus acquired section 21, and at Melrose the brewery was owned by the Jacka family from Wadebridge. At Orroroo the Cornish colonists included James Teague, who settled on section 66, and John Arthur, who had been a miner at Tungkillo in the Adelaide Hills before purchasing 640 acres in the district. There was also Richard Ellery, born at Tywardreath in 1844, who had in earlier days worked in the Burra and at the Blinman, Prince Alfred and Sliding Rock mines in the Far North. Christopher Williams, who had 991 acres in the district, had once been employed in the Wallaroo Mines, and Samuel Carter from St Agnes had been a storekeeper at Kapunda and at Jamestown before purchasing the general-store at Orroroo. Thirty miles to the west, at Beautiful Valley (later Wilmington) was Thomas Harris, a former Burra and Moonta miner, and Samuel Hill from the parish of Kenwyn.

This dispersal of the South Australian population into the new agricultural areas in the 1870s was accompanied, as one would expect, by a new upsurge in Methodist chapel-building, and the development of social life in these areas—literary societies, institutes, even newspapers—was due in part to the Methodist influence. As ever, the Cornish settlers were in the forefront of this activity, and again a brief catalogue of personalities and their involvement in Methodist expansion gives some indication of the extent to which that was true.

At Laura, the Bryants from Hayle pioneered the growth of local Methodism aided by Henry Nicholls from Helston and W. H. Binney—a Cornishman who had moved from Willunga to take up land along the Rocky River in 1872. At Jamestown, a certain Mrs Williams was responsible for laying the foundation stone of the local Wesleyan chapel which, according to the enthusiastic description in the *Australian Christian Commonwealth* magazine in June 1908, ". . . was long regarded as the cathedral of Methodism in the North . . .", one of its leading members for more than thirty years being Walter Treleaven from Nanstallon. When Thomas Hosking moved from Clare to Terowie in 1873 he became treasurer of the newly-established Wesleyan chapel, while a Mrs Pomeroy from Crowan was similarly active at nearby Petersburg (later Peterborough). And when, in 1877, Henry Waters from Penzance selected land in the Hundred of Booleroo, he became a trustee of the first Bible Christian chapel in the district—it being said that the first sermon at Booleroo Centre was preached from the back of a wagon that he had especially lent for the purpose! In the same way, William Nottle from Probus played an important role in the establishment of the Baptist denomination in the districts surrounding Booleroo. At Orroroo, Samuel Carter from St Agnes was a prominent Methodist, while Ann Moyle from Breage was instrumental in the foundation of the Bible Christian chapel at Carrieton after she and her husband arrived in the district in 1879.

Of all the religious denominations, the Methodists—whether Bible Christians, Wesleyans or Primitive Methodists—were the best equipped to exploit the colonising process, requiring neither fixed buildings nor paid clergy in the early stages of expansion, and relying on their own "self-help" activities to finance their local societies. However, the rapid expansion of the northern wheat frontier in the 1870s, and the consequent dramatic increase in the number of preaching places, meant that even the Methodists were hard-pushed to serve their "flocks" in the far-flung Far North. It was clear that more ordained Ministers were required urgently in the colony if the momentum of expansion was to be maintained. As early as 1873 the Bible Christians had seven Ministers in the North—the Revs James Trewin, John Dingle, George Henry Paynter, William Richards, Thomas Piper, William Wesley Finch, and John Thorne. Of these, James Trewin had worked in Kilkhampton circuit before migrating to South Australia and John Thorne, a member of the celebrated

Thorne family of Shebbear in North Devon, had worked amongst the Cornish miners on Yorke Peninsula. John Dingle was a Cornishman, as was George Henry Paynter from Hick's Mill, Gwennap, who, according to one account, was ". . . the first to hold services and build churches in towns and neighbourhoods in that part of the state", being Secretary of the South Australian Bush Mission for 40 years.

But despite their efforts, there was a requirement for further trained guidance in the new agricultural districts, and in 1876 the Bible Christian Conference—held in Zion Chapel, St Austell—had no less than 297 vacancies to fill in Australasia. The Rev. John Thorne was in Cornwall to address the Conference and to put the case for South Australia. The *Bible Christian Magazine* recorded that,

> Br. John Thorne spoke with great ability on the claims of South Australia and of the great need there was for more missionaries to carry on the work in that important colony. "But", said Mr Thorne, "some say you can't get anyone to go; but that to me is not a satisfactory answer. I want to know why you do not go yourselves? (laughter, and loud applause). We don't want you to get anyone else, come yourselves".

Thorne's direct and humerous style was successful to some degree in winning new recruits for South Australia and her wheat frontier. Richard Carlyon Yeoman, who was born in Illogan but had lived for many years at Perranwell, had already been persuaded to take the step and after his arrival in the colony worked first of all in the Port Wakefield Circuit, but then moving to ". . . the newly opened northern areas . . ." where, according to the obituary notes in the Conference Minutes for 1924, he ". . . did much to establish the Methodist Church among the pioneer settlers".

Two other Bible Christian Ministers to arrive in South Australia in this period were the Revs William Francis James and William Thomas Penrose. Penrose was born at Tregurno in the parish of St Buryan in 1850, in 1863 preaching his first sermon (in Drift chapel), and in 1870 becoming a local preacher in St Just Circuit under the direction of the Rev. J. Raymont (the Devon-born Minister who later also volunteered for South

Australia). He spent two years as a hired local preacher in the Scillies, but by the time he arrived in South Australia in the 1880s he was an ordained Minister. He went first to Snowtown, and from there into the heart of the northern districts to minister to the frontier pioneers. W. F. James, from Truro, was ordained in 1872 and was in his day regarded as one of the most successful preachers in Cornwall. He emigrated to South Austraia in the early 1880s, in response to the urgent need for Missionaries, working amongst the northern farmers and eventually becoming President of the Bible Christian Conference in the colony.

The Wesleyans, too, could boast several Cornish pioneers in the Far North. The Rev. John Hosking Trevorrow, born at Lelant in 1836, preached at the Blinman mine and in the surrounding districts, while the Rev. John Grenfell Jenkin worked in the border country of South Australia's Far North and New South Wales' Barrier Ranges. The Rev. Hugh Henwood Teague was born at St Issey in 1851. In 1873 he commenced training as a Minister for the Wesleyan Foreign Mission Society and, after three years' study, he was sent to South Australia where he took up duties at Port Pirie. There his work entailed riding many miles on horseback through wild and unfriendly country, often in the heat of the day, to reach isolated families in the new areas. As a result of his over-exertions, his health failed and he was sent back to Cornwall to recuperate. By 1878 he was again in the colony, taking up where he had left off before and becoming a senior member of the Wesleyan Church. He was twice secretary of the Conference, became editor of the *Christian Weekly and Methodist Journal*, and was well known for his lively lectures on "Cornwall and the Cornish". His colleague, the Rev. James Allen, born at Roche in 1840, was also instrumental in the northern expansion—being stationed for some time at Jamestown—and the Rev. John Leggoe, from St Just, was similarly important.

By the early 1880s, then, the northward expansion of the wheat frontier had brought many Cornish families to the Far North region, where they played a significant part in clearing the land and establishing farms, setting up new townships and their attendent industries, and moulding the social and religious life of these new districts. But even in 1880 there were the first signs that all might not be well, that natural law did not dictate that rain must folow the plough, a hint that the expansion of the 1870s had been too great—taking those intensely, almost naively optimistic settlers to lands where rainfall was too light and too inconsistent to support close settlement and agriculture.

17. A stripper made by May Brothers of Gawler and used on the South Australian wheat frontier in the 1890s. Courtesy Jim Faull.

The rainfall in 1880 was unusually light, leading to the failure of crops in some of the northern districts, but 1881 was worse—the prelude to a long drought which afflicted South Australia for a decade, coinciding with a general economic downturn which ushered in a period of depression and brought an end to the colony's immigration policies. As the drought began to bite, so the agricultural frontier began to retreat, luckless farmers abandoning their properties as their crops failed and their animals died. The number of flocks and herds declined sharply, and wheat production collapsed in many areas. In the Carrieton-Hawker region, for example, as R. M. Gibbs shows in his *A History of South Australia*, the average yield per acre of wheat (in bushels) was 10.9 in 1878 but had fallen dramatically to 1.6 in 1881. The total wheat production in the colony fell from 14.2 million bushels in 1879 to 7.35 million in 1882. In all, some 600,000 acres of land were abandoned in that decade, a terrible experience not only for the individual farmers concerned but also for the colony as a whole. The seemingly unbeatable expansionist spirit of the 1870s was now sadly dented, and with it something of the colony's self-confidence and vision was diminished. Northern properties reverted to semi-desert, farm houses once teeming with activity soon became empty, roofless shells, boundary fences were blown down or smothered by salt-bush, and here and there "ghost towns" became eerie landmarks upon the northern expanses. The agony and sense of despair experienced by some of these settlers in the 1880s was conveyed in a letter written by Walter Treloar (a son of Francis Treloar, who emigrated to Australia from Penryn in 1842) to his brother Frank:

> Well, the drought continues, and I am here on the station with a black boy, everybody has gone long ago. This I am sending by a passing black boy to Charlotte. Cattle and horses are dead everywhere in thousands. All outside waters are dry, and the few alive are dependent on the "Pool" which is nearly dry. I have about three weeks flour left and very litte else. Never did I dream we should reach this. Arthur and I are ruined men, having lost everything.

The contraction of the northern frontier had important social consequences. Many of those literary societies and institutes founded in the enthusiastic '70s were abandoned, and the Methodists found much of their earlier work threatened. Already hit by the closure of the mines at Kapunda and Burra Burra, and the departure of Cornish miners from Yorke Peninsula to go to the newly-discovered Broken Hill silver fields, the Methodists became aware that their future in South Australia—their "own" colony, the original "Paradise of Dissent"—was not as assured as they had assumed it to be only a few years before. On paper, the Methodists were still strong in the 1880s. Their combined strength was amost 63,300—comprising nearly 42,100 Wesleyans, 10,900 Bible Christians (mostly drawn from the Cornish community), 10,300 Primitive Methodists (20 per cent of whom lived on norhern Yorke Peninsula), and 400 New

Connexion Methodists. But despite their apparent numerical strength, the Methodists were suffering increasingly from the effects of the economic climate, the smaller denominations in particular facing the prospect of declining chapel attendance and growing financial difficulties.

A report compiled by the Bible Christians in the early 1880s blamed the scattered nature of the rural population for all the problems, pointing to a lack of co-operation between preachers and laity, and criticising the deleterious effects of competition between the various denominations. In earlier days the competitive spirit that had existed between the denominations had been an impetus to expansion, but in the atmosphere of the 1880s it led only to duplication and a waste of valuable resources. With the realisation that such duplication was counter-productive, the movement towards Methodist Union in South Australia was set in motion. Union took some twenty years to achieve, and it was a difficult task in the extreme, but in the end the denominations resolved their differences, and—in 1900—formal Union was achieved, breathing new vigour into the Methodist Church and assuring it of a prominent place in twentieth-century South Australia. Interestingly, despite much grass-roots opposition to Union amongst the Cornish (especially from the Bible Christians), some of the strongest advocates of Union were Cornish Ministers—such as the Rev. James Rowe from Penzance, one of the original Bible Christian preachers in the colony, and the Rev. W. F. James from Truro who was ". . . one of the prime movers in Methodist Union . . .".

Just as the Methodists reacted to the contraction of the northern wheat frontier and the consequent problems with pragmatism and innovation, so the rest of South Australian society readjusted to the new conditions. Economic belts were tightened, assisted immigration was halted, and the lessons of Goyder's line were relearned. In particular, it was realised that new techniques would have to be developed if the marginal lands were to be farmed successfully, and in 1881 an experimental farm (later college) was established at Roseworthy, near Gawler. The farm experimented with fertilisers and it encouraged the use of super-phosphate, an innovation that save many South Australian farmers—Cornish among them—especially on Yorke Peninsula and in the Far North. Thus, while the frontier did indeed retreat, many settlers did manage to survive the drought of the 1880s, and even today—in districts such as Booleroo, Orroroo and Jamestown—one still finds farming families with the tell-tale Cornish surnames, living testament to the courage and tenacity of their nineteenth-cenury forebears.

# *Retrospect*

Should, at the turn of the century, Edward Gibbon Wakefield have been able to review the progress of the colony of South Australia over the previous sixty-odd years, we can be confident that—although the "finished product" was no doubt rather different from the model envisaged by the early enthusiasts for "systematic colonisation"—he would have been well-pleased with what he saw. South Australia was still recognisably "different" when compared to the other Antipodean settlements, especially the neighbouring colonies of Victoria and New South Wales, and its population of Protestant "self-made" men still reflected the colony's early nonconformist flavour. The Rev. John Blacket, the colony's Methodist historian, was in 1899 in a position to reflect upon South Australia's development, and wrote that:

> We have seen the first colonist (Samuel Stephens) put his foot on Australian shore. We have seen the early emigrants' tents pitched amongst the trees and rushes that skirted the shores of Holdfast Bay. Beds made of rushes; pork barrells and packing cases extemperised as tables; emigrants dragging their goods to the site of a city that was yet to be, have passed before our view. Where those tents, sixty-two years ago, were pitched, the large and aristocratic town of Glenelg now stands, which has some of the finest streets that the Southern Hemisphere can show, and its system of deep drainage is unsurpassed. Trams are running in all directions. Through country that sixty years ago was unexplored and unknown, trains now rush, laden with passengers, wheat, wool, sheep, cattle, and mineral wealth. There is a beautiful park around the city; outside are crowded suburbs. The population in and around Adelaide alone has been estimated at about one hundred thousand. Dotted over the country are towns, villages, gardens and farms. It seems like a fairy tale. All has been accomplished in less than three score years and ten. Sixty-two years ago the population was about five hundred; today it is more than three hundred thousand.

In all this, as we have seen, Cornish folk played an important role. As Pascoe wrote in 1901, ". . . the energy and ambition of Cornishmen found for them prominence in colonial public affairs and commerical life"—the notable Stephens family amongst the founding fathers, the great men like Boucaut and Bonython, engineers and craftsmen such as James Martin and Nicholas Wallis Trudgen. But it remains the case that the great bulk of Cornish migrants were "ordinary" folk, working men and their wives and children, and it is their contribution to the expansion of Adelaide and the South Australian agricultural frontier that is most noticeable and most impressive.

# Select Bibliography

## ARCHIVAL SOURCES

(a)*Helston Museum*
2290 John Boaden, *Some Account of My Life and Times*, 1902–4

(b)*Royal Institution of Cornwall*
Extracts from the *West Briton* and *Royal Cornwall Gazette* relating to Cornish emigration in the nineteenth century.
*Posters* relating to emigration from Cornwall to South Australia.

(c)*South Australian Archives*

| | |
|---|---|
| 97/379-98u | *Boucaut Papers* |
| 124 | *Report on the Bible Christians of South Australia,* c1881. |
| 313 | *Passenger Lists* |
| 921u | *Contract Between the South Australian Railway Commissioners and James Martin & Co. Ltd. for the Supply of 92 locomotives,* 26 August 1891. |
| 1047 | *Biographical Notes.* |
| 1209 | Rodney Cockburn, *Nomenclature of South Australia* (Revised Version). |
| 1497 | Bentham MSS, *Notes on Colonization Proposals for South Australia* (copies only, originals in University of London). |
| 1529 | *Alphabetical Index to Applications for Free Passage from the United Kingdom to South Australia 1836–40.* |
| D4066(L) | Richard Jagoe, *The Cruise of the S.S. Governor Musgrave from February 15 to February 27 1893.* |
| D5013(T) | G. Barzon, *The Pirates and Wreckers of Kangaroo Island,* 1895. |
| D5069(Misc) | *Sermons written and delivered by the Rev. John Langdon Parsons, some-time of the Baptist Church, Tynte Street, 1860s and 1870s.* |
| D5422(Misc) | *Sermon Notes by John L. Parsons.* |
| D5633(T) | Malcolm Vaughan, *The Development of Agriculture and the Slate Industry in the Willunga Area in the nineteenth century.* |
| D5857(Misc) | Edith Casely, *History of the Trudgen Family in South Australia.* |
| D6018(T) | Meryl A. Kuchel, *Pies and Pasties: A Cornish Community in an Australian Environment,* 1976. |
| D6029/1-115(L) | *Letters written home by Cornish folk who emigrated to Australia in the nineteenth-century,* collected by John M. Tregenza. |

| PRG 125 | Papers of John N. Stephens relating to the Stephens Family. |
| PRG 174 | George Fife Angas Papers. |
| RN 16 | Notes on George Marsden Waterhouse. |
| RN 201 | A Few Notes on the History of Nairne. |
| RN 260 | Some Notable Cornish Pioneers. |

## NEWSPAPERS & PERIODICALS

(a) *British*
Bible Christian Magazine
Commercial, Shipping and General Advertiser for West Cornwall
Cornishman
Cornish Magazine
Primitive Methodist Magazine
Royal Cornwall Gazette
South Australian News
South Australian Record
Wesleyan Methodist Magazine
West Briton

(b) *Australian*
Australian Christian Commonwealth
Christian Weekly and Methodist Journal
Observer (Adelaide)
People's Weekly
South Australian Advertiser
South Australian Primitive Methodist
South Australian Register
Yorke's Peninsula Advertiser

## BOOKS, PAMPHLETS & ARTICLES

| Anon, | Forty Years President: Complimentary Dinner to the Hon. Sir J. Langdon Bonython, School of Mines, Adelaide, 1936. |
| Ian Auhl, | Burra and District: A Pictorial Memoir, Lynton, Adelaide, 1975. |
| Ian Auhl, | From Settlement to City: A History of the District of Tea Tree Gully, 1836–1976, Lynton, Adelaide, 1976. |

*Australian Dictionary of Biography*, Melbourne University Press, Melbourne, 6 Vols., 1966–76.

| R. M. Barton, | Life in Cornwall in the Nineteenth-Century, D. Bradford Barton, Truro, 4 Vols., 1970–74. |

| John Blacket, | *A South Australian Romance: How a Colony was Founded and a Methodist Church Formed*, 1899. |
|---|---|
| John Blacket, | *History of South Australia: A Romantic and Successful Experiment in Colonization*, Hussey & Gillingham, Adelaide, 1911. |
| Liz Blieschke, | *Plain of Contrast: A History of Willowie-Amyton-Booleroo Whim*, District Centenary Book Committee, Booleroo Whim, 1975. |
| Eric Glenie Bonython, | *History of the families of Bonython of Bonython and Bonython of Carclew in the Duchy of Cornwall*, published privately, Adelaide, 1966. |
| John Langdon Bonython, | *Cornwall: Interesting History and Romantic Stories*, Advertiser, Adelaide, 1932. |
| James Penn Boucaut, | *Letters to My Boys*, Gay & Bird, London, 1906. |
| F. W. Bourne, | *The Bible Christians: Their Origins and History*, Bible Christian Book Room, London, 1905. |
| Charles Wesley Bowden, | *History of Agery*, Bowden, Agery, 1966. |
| J. Britton and E. W. Brayley, | *Cornwall Illustrated in a Series of Views*, 1831, republished, D. Bradford Barton, Truro, 1968. |
| Arthur Burfield, | *Booleroo Times: A History of the Hundred of Booleroo 1875–1975* Booleroo Centre Book Committee, Booleroo Centre, 1975. |
| H. T. Burgess (Ed.), | *The Cyclopedea of South Australia*, 2 Vols., Alfred G. Selway, Adelaide, 1907 |
| Henry Farnham Burke, | *History of the Family of Bonython of Bonython in the Duchy of Cornwall*, Harrison & Sons, London, 1926. |
| Arnold Caldicott | *The Verco Story: Hopes We Live By*, Caldicott, Adelaide, Adelaide, 1970. |
| Ern Carmichael, | *The Ill-Shaped Leg: A Story of the Development of Yorke Peninsula*, Carmichael, Adelaide, 1973. |
| Ern Carmichael, | *Yorke Peninsula Sketchbook*, Rigby, Adelaide, 1972. |
| Rodney Cockburn, | *Pastoral Pioneers of South Australia*, 2 Vols., 1925, republished, Lynton, Adelaide, 1974. |
| G. D. Combe, | *Responsible Government in South Australia*, S.A. Government, Adelaide, 1957. |
| E. H. Coombe, | *History of Gawler 1837–1908*, Gawler Institute, Gawler, 1910. |
| Henry Cornish, | *Under the Southern Cross*, 1890, republished, Penguin, Ringwood, 1975. |
| P. R. Dunlop, | "Economic Importance of Moonta to South Australia", *Proceedings of History of Moonta Seminar*, Yorke Peninsula Adult Education Centre and National Trust of S.A. (Moonta Branch), Moonta, 1970. |
| Martin Dunstan, | *Willunga: Town and District 1837–1900*, Lynton, Adelaide, 1977. |

| | |
|---|---|
| Charles Fenner, | *South Australia: A Geographic Study*, Whitcombe & Tombs, Sydney, 1931. |
| Stanley G. Forth | *Methodism in the Clare District*, South Australian Methodist Historical Society, Adelaide, 1974. |
| R. M. Gibbs, | *History of South Australia*, Balara Books, Adelaide, 1969. |
| William Harcus (Ed.), | *South Australia: Its History, Resources and Production*, 1876. |
| J. B. Hirst, | *Adelaide and Country 1870–1917: Their Social and Political Relationship*, Melbourne University Press, Melbourne, 1973. |
| Edwin Hodder, | *The History of South Australia From Its Foundation To the Year of its Jublilee*, 2 Vols., 1893. |
| L. Hughes et al, | *Beautiful Valley: A History of Wilmington and District 1876–1976*, Hughes, Wilmington, 1976. |
| Fred. Jones, | *The Honourable Sir Langdon Bonython KCMG: An Eminent Australian*, Royal Cornwall Polytechnic Society, Camborne, 1931. |
| W. S. Kelly, | *Rural Development in South Australia*, Rigby, Adelaide, 1962. |
| John King-Roach, | *Not Without Courage*, Hawke & Co., Kapunda, 1957. |
| R. A. C. and T. E. Knowling, | *A History of Mundulla and its People*, Mundulla Centenary Committee, Munulla, 1973. |
| George E. Loyau, | *Notable South Australians, or Colonists—Past and Present*, 1885, republished, Austaprint, Adelaide, 1978. |
| George E. Loyau, | *The Representative Men of South Australia*, 1883, republished, Austaprint, Adelaide, 1978. |
| Tony Lucas, | *Willunga Profile*, Lantern Black, Sydney, 1972. |
| Lillie Mayhew, | "The Pioneering Life of James and Elizabeth Harvey—Buffalo Pioneers", *South Australian Geneologist*, Vol. 2, No. 1, Summer 1975. |
| D. W. Meinig, | *On the Margins of the Good Earth: The Expansion of the South Australian Wheat Frontier 1869–1884*, Seal, Adelaide, 1970. |
| Mary Mills, | *Millbrae and its Founding Family*, published privately, Adelaide, 1973. |
| J. V. Morgan, | *Colonial Methodism in South Australia*, Lynton, Aelaide, 1973. |
| W. Frederick Morrison, | *Th Aldine History of South Australia*, 1890. |
| Jean V. Moyle, | *The Wakefield: Its Water and Wealth*, Moyle, Riverton, 1975. |
| Nancy Parnell, | *Orroroo: Rendezvous of the Magpie*, Orroroo Centenary Committee, Orroroo, 1975. |
| J. J. Pascoe, | *History of Adelaide and Vicinity*, 1901, republished, Osterstock, Adelaide, 1972. |

| | |
|---|---|
| Philip Payton, | *Pictorial History of Australia's Little Cornwall*, Rigby, Adelaide, 1978. |
| Philip Payton, | *The Cornish Miner in Australia: Cousin Jack Down Under*, Dyllansow Truran, Redruth, 1984. |
| Philip Payton, | *Cornish Carols From Australia*, Dyllansow Truran, Redruth, 1984. |
| Douglas Pike, | *Paradise of Dissent: South Australia 1827–1857*, Longmans, London, 1957. |
| Oswald Pryor, | *Australia's Little Cornwall*, Rigby, Adelaide, 1962. |
| John Reynolds, | *Men and Mines: A History of Australian Mining 1788–1971*, Sun Books, Melbourne, 1974. |
| Nancy Robinson, | *Change on Change: A History of the Northern Highlands of South Australia*, Investigator Press, Adelaide, 1971. |
| John Rowe, | *The Hard-Rock Men: Cornish Immigrants and the North American Mining Frontier*, University of Liverpool Press, Liverpool, 1973. |
| A. L. Rowse, | *The Cornish in America*, Macmillan, London, 1969 |
| Heather Sizer, | *Yet Still They Live: Wirrabarra's Story*, Sizer, Wirrabarra, 1974. |
| Phyllis Somerville, | "The Influence of Cornwall on South Australian Methodism", *Journal of the South Australian Methodist Historical Society*, Volume 4, October 1972. |
| John Stephens, | *The Land of Promise: Being an Authentic and Impartial History of the Rise and Progress of the New British Province of South Australia*, 1839. |
| Harold J. Stowe, | *They Built Strathalbyn*, Investigator Press, Adelaide, 1973. |
| Charles Sturt, | *Two Expeditions into the Interior of Australia*, 2 Vols., 1833. |
| George Sutherland, | *The South Australian Company: A Study in Colonisation*, 1898. |
| H. R. Taylor, | *The History of the Churches of Christ in South Australia*, The Churches of Christ Evangelical Union, Adelaide, 1959. |
| A. C. Todd, | *The Cornish Miner in America*, D. Bradford Barton, Truro, 1967. |
| A. C. Todd, | *The Search for Silver: Cornish Miners in Mexico*, Lodenek Press, Padstow, 1977. |
| P. W. Verco, | *Masons, Millers and Medicine: James Crabb Verco and his Sons*, Verco, Adelaide, 1976. |
| E. Gibbon Wakefield, | *A View of the Art of Colonization*, 1849. |
| Gladys Ward, | *The Yongala Story*, Lynton, Adelaide, 1974. |
| Derek Whitelock, | *Adelaide 1836–1976: A History of Difference*, University of Queensland Press, St Lucia, 1977. |

| Ken Whitford, | *Yankalilla and District Sketchbook*, Rigby, Adelaide, 1974. |
| Michael Williams, | *The Making of the South Australian Landscape*, Academic Press, London, 1974. |

# UNIVERSITY OF ADELAIDE UNPUBLISHED THESES

| John Barrett, | "The Union of the Methodist Churches in South Australia: A Preliminary Survey of Official Action and Expressed Opinion 1881–1900", BA Hons., 1955. |
| K. W. A. Bray, | "Government-Sponsored Immigration into South Australia 1872–86", MA, 1961. |
| Kay Y. Connolly, | "A Preliminary Survey of Methodism, its Growth, Influence and Culture in South Australia 1836–1901", BA Hons., 1976. |
| P. L. Edgar, | "Sir James Penn Boucaut His Political Life 1861–75", BA Hons., 1961. |
| S. G. Fitzgerald, | "Half a World Away: South Australian Migration 1851–1872", BA Hons., 1969. |
| Philip Payton, | "The Cornish in South Australia: Their Influence and Experience From Immigration to Assimilation 1836–1936", PhD, 1978. |
| B. M. H. Reynolds, | "Immigration into South Australia 1829–52", Tinline, 1928. |

# MISCELLANEOUS SOURCES

Jim Faull Collection of Cornish obituaries from the *Christian Weekly and Methodist Journal*, held by Jim Faull of the S.A. College of Advanced Education.

G. E. Middleton, *History of Willamulka*, unpublished paper of 1929 in private collection of Roslyn Paterson, Bute, South Australia.

*Minutes of the Cornish Association of South Australia.*

*Minutes of the South Australian Conference of the Methodist Church of Australia.*

*Miscellaneous Reports of the Missionary Society Under the Direction of the Bible Christian Conference.*

*South Australian Almanacks, Directories and Gazeteers.*

*South Austraian Parliamentary Debates.*

*South Australian Parliamentary Papers.*

# APPENDIX 1

IMMIGRATION INTO SOUTH AUSTRALIA, AS CALCULATED FROM S.A.A. 1529, ALPHABETICAL INDEX TO APPLICATIONS FOR FREE PASSAGE FROM THE UNITED KINGDOM TO SOUTH AUSTRALIA 1836–40, AND S.A.A. 313 PASSENGER LISTS

(a)

| Years | Cornish Applications | Total Applications | Cornish Applications Approved (Estimated) | Total Applications Approved |
|---|---|---|---|---|
| 1836–40 | 941 | 9,422 | 507 | 5,070 |

| Years | Estimated Cornish Immigration | Total Immigration | Percentage Cornish |
|---|---|---|---|
| 1836–40 | 1,400 | 14,000 | 10 |

(b)

| Year | Cornish Immigration | Total Immigration | Percentage Cornish | Number of miners |
|---|---|---|---|---|
| 1836–40 | 1,400 | 14,000 | 10.0 | |
| 1845 | 24 | 168 | 14.3 | |
| 1846 | 29 | 55 | 52.7 | |
| 1847 | — | — | — | |
| 1848 | 44 | 249 | 17.7 | |
| 1849 | 778 | 6,335 | 12.3 | |
| 1850 | 221 | 2,790 | 7.9 | |
| 1851 | 465 | 3,588 | 13.0 | |
| 1852 | 228 | 5,044 | 4.5 | |
| 1853 | 444 | 4,757 | 9.3 | |
| 1854 | 929 | 8,866 | 10.5 | |
| 1855 | 713 | 10,928 | 6.5 | |
| 1856 | 560 | 4,962 | 11.3 | |
| 1857 | 1,122 | 3,920 | 28.6 | |
| 1858 | 441 | 4,102 | 10.8 | |
| 1859 | 130 | 1,753 | 7.4 | |
| 1860 | 103 | 966 | 10.7 | |

## (b) continued.

| Year | Cornish Immigration | Total Immigration | Percentage Cornish | Number of miners |
|------|--------------------:|------------------:|-------------------:|-----------------:|
| 1861 | — | — | — | |
| 1862 | 5 | 305 | 1.6 | |
| 1863 | 183 | 1,494 | 12.2 | |
| 1864 | 426 | 2,641 | 16.1 | |
| 1865 | 1,982 | 4,655 | 42.5 | |
| 1866 | 479 | 3,326 | 14.4 | |
| 1867 | 152 | 786 | 19.3 | |
| 1868 | — | — | — | |
| 1869 | 8 | 58 | 13.8 | |
| 1870 | — | — | — | |
| 1871 | — | — | — | |
| 1872 | — | — | — | |
| 1873 | 38 | 226 | 16.8 | 3 |
| 1874 | 185 | 1,835 | 10.1 | 62 |
| 1875 | 79 | 2,030 | 3.9 | 29 |
| 1876 | 589 | 7,737 | 7.6 | 198 |
| 1877 | 379 | 5,064 | 7.5 | 84 |
| 1878 | 277 | 4,258 | 6.5 | 3 |
| 1879 | 132 | 3,189 | 4.1 | 0 |
| 1880 | 29 | 794 | 3.7 | 0 |
| 1881 | 48 | 772 | 6.2 | 1 |
| 1882 | 48 | 1,113 | 4.3 | 1 |
| 1883 | 241 | 3,891 | 6.2 | 64 |
| 1884 | 48 | 880 | 5.5 | 1 |
| 1885 | — | — | — | — |
| 1886 | 8 | 293 | 2.7 | — |
| TOTALS | 12,967 | 162,853 | 8.0 | 446 |

# APPENDIX 2

## THE POPULATION OF SOUTH AUSTRALIA 1836–1900

*Source: Statistical Register of The State of South Australia for the Year 1914, South Australian Parliamentary Papers, 1915.*

| Year | Population |
|------|------------|
| 1836 | 546 |
| 1837 | — |
| 1838 | 6,000 |
| 1839 | — |
| 1840 | 14,630 |
| 1841 | — |
| 1842 | — |
| 1843 | 17,196 |
| 1844 | 18,999 |
| 1845 | 22,460 |
| 1846 | 25,893 |
| 1847 | 31,153 |
| 1848 | 38,666 |
| 1849 | 52,904 |
| 1850 | 63,700 |
| 1851 | 66,538 |
| 1852 | 68,663 |
| 1853 | 78,944 |
| 1854 | 92,545 |
| 1855 | 97,387 |
| 1856 | 107,886 |
| 1857 | 109,917 |
| 1858 | 118,665 |
| 1859 | 122,735 |
| 1860 | 124,112 |
| 1861 | 130,627 |
| 1862 | 135,329 |
| 1863 | 140,416 |
| 1864 | 147,341 |
| 1865 | 156,605 |
| 1866 | 169,153 |
| 1867 | 172,860 |
| 1868 | 176,298 |
| 1869 | 181,146 |
| 1870 | 183,797 |
| 1871 | 188,817 |
| 1872 | 192,022 |

| Year | Population |
|------|-----------|
| 1873 | 197,874 |
| 1874 | 204,422 |
| 1875 | 210,241 |
| 1876 | 224,934 |
| 1877 | 236,121 |
| 1878 | 248,052 |
| 1879 | 258,544 |
| 1880 | 266,830 |
| 1881 | 282,873 |
| 1882 | 189,096 |
| 1883 | 289,096 |
| 1884 | 307,433 |
| 1885 | 306,212 |
| 1886 | 304,336 |
| 1887 | 308,215 |
| 1888 | 306,641 |
| 1889 | 311,112 |
| 1890 | 314,195 |
| 1891 | 319,804 |
| 1892 | 329,650 |
| 1893 | 338,912 |
| 1894 | 343,237 |
| 1895 | 346,716 |
| 1896 | 347,252 |
| 1897 | 348,117 |
| 1898 | 350,877 |
| 1899 | 354,935 |
| 1900 | 357,099 |

# APPENDIX 3

APPLICATIONS FOR FREE PASSAGE FROM CORNWALL TO SOUTH AUSTRALIA, 1836–40, ANALYSED ACCORDING TO SEX, YEAR OF APPLICATION, OCCUPATION AND PARISH (10 TABLES)

*Source:* S.A.A. 1529, *Alphabetical Index to Applications for Free Passage from the United Kingdom to South Australia, 1836–40.*

*Note:* For the most part traditional ecclesiastical Cornish parish boundaries have been adhered to, except in some instances (e.g. Camelford) where modern civil boundaries make for greater clarity.

TABLE 1. 1836, Applications for Free Passage from Cornwall to South Australia, MALES, by Occupation and Parish

| Parish | Agric. Labourer/ Gardener | Carpenter | Labourer | Sheep-Shearer | Totals |
|--------|---------------------------|-----------|----------|---------------|--------|
| Falmouth |  |  | 1 |  | 1 |
| Madron |  | 1 |  |  | 1 |
| Sancreed |  |  |  | 1 | 1 |
| St Levan |  | 1 |  |  | 1 |
| Warleggan | 1 |  |  |  | 1 |
| TOTALS | 1 | 2 | 1 | 1 | 5 Grand Total |

TABLE 2. 1837, Applications for Free Passage from Cornwall to South Australia, MALES, by Occupation and Parish

| | Agricultural Labourer/Gardener | Blacksmith | Butcher | Carpenter | Farmer/Husbandman | Harness-maker | Labourer | Mason | Miner | Plasterer | Servant | Shoemaker | Tailor | Totals |
|---|---|---|---|---|---|---|---|---|---|---|---|---|---|---|
| Altarnun | | | | | | | 1 | | | | | | | 1 |
| Budock | 1 | | | | | | | | | | | | | 1 |
| Callington | | 1 | | 2 | | | | | | | | 1 | | 4 |
| Falmouth | | | | | | | | 3 | | 1 | 1 | 2 | | 7 |
| Gwennap | | | | | 1 | | 10 | | 1 | | | 1 | | 13 |
| Illogan | | | | | | | 2 | | 3 | | | | | 5 |
| Lanteglos-by-Fowey | | | | | | | | | | | | 1 | | 1 |
| Launceston | | | | 3 | 1 | | | 2 | | | | | | 6 |
| Lewannick | | | | 1 | | | 1 | | | | | | | 2 |
| Linkinhorne | 1 | | | | | | 2 | | | | | | | 3 |
| Mylor | 1 | | | | | | | | | | | | | 1 |
| North Hill | | | | | | 1 | 1 | | | | | | | 2 |
| Penryn | 1 | | 2 | 1 | 1 | 2 | | 1 | | | | 1 | | 9 |
| Redruth | | | | | 1 | | 4 | | | | | | | 5 |
| St Austell | | 1 | | | | | 1 | | 1 | | | | | 3 |
| St Blazey | | | | | | | | | 1 | | | | | 1 |
| St Breward | 2 | | | | | | 3 | 1 | | | | | | 6 |
| St Mawgan¹ | | | | 2 | | | | | | | | | | 1 |
| Stithians | | | | | 1 | | | | | | | | | 1 |
| Truro | | | | 1 | | | | | | | | | 1 | 2 |
| Tywardreath | | 1 | | | | | 1 | | | | | | | 2 |
| Totals | 6 | 3 | 2 | 8 | 6 | 4 | 26 | 7 | 6 | 1 | 1 | 6 | 1 | 79 |

¹—Probably St Mawgan-in-Pydar

Grand
Total

119

## TABLE 3. 1838, Applications for Free Passage from Cornwall

| | Agricultural Labourer/Gardener | Blacksmith | Butcher | Cardwainer | Carman | Carpenter | Cooper | Farmer/Husbandman | Fisherman | Glazier | Harness-maker |
|---|---|---|---|---|---|---|---|---|---|---|---|
| Altarnun | 1 | | | | | | | | | | |
| Antony | 1 | | | | | | | | | | |
| Bodmin | | | | | | | | | | | |
| Calstock | | | | | | | | 1 | | | 1 |
| Camborne | | | | | | | | 1 | | | |
| Creed | | | | | | | | 2 | | | |
| Crowan | | | | | | | | 3 | | | |
| Falmouth | | | | | 1 | 2 | 1 | | 1 | | |
| Fowey | 1 | | | | | | | | | | |
| Gwennap | 5 | 1 | | 1 | | | | 5 | | 1 | |
| Hayle | | | | | | | | | | | |
| Helston | | | | | | | | 1 | | | |
| Kea | 1 | | | | | | | | | | |
| Kenwyn | 1 | | | | | | | | | | |
| Launceston | | | 1 | | | | | | | | |
| Linkinhorne | 1 | | | | | 1 | | | | | |
| Mawnan | | | | | | | | 1 | | | |
| Mevagissey | 1 | | | | | | | | | | |
| Mylor | 6 | | | | | | | 3 | | | |
| Penryn | | | | | | 1 | 1 | 2 | | | |
| Perranarworthal | | | | | | | | | | | |
| Probus | | | | | | | | | | | |
| Ruanlanihorne | | | | | | | | | | | |
| St Agnes | | | | | | | | | | | |
| St Austell | | | | | | | | | | | |
| St Blazey | | | | | | 2 | | 1 | | | |
| St Clether | 1 | | | | | | | | | | |
| St Dominick | | 1 | | | | | | | | | |
| St Ewe | | | | | | | | | | | |
| St Gluvias | | | | | | | | | | | |
| St Mawgan[1] | 1 | | | | | | | 3 | | | |
| St Stephen[2] | | | | | | 1 | | | | | |
| South Petherwin | | | | | | | | | | | |
| Towednack | | | | | | 1 | | 3 | | | |
| Tregony | 1 | | | | | | | 1 | | | |
| Tresmeer | 1 | | | | | | | | | | |
| Truro | | 1 | | | | 1 | | | | | |
| Wendron | | | | | | | | 1 | | | |
| **Totals** | 22 | 3 | 1 | 1 | 1 | 8 | 2 | 28 | 1 | 1 | 1 |

[1]—Probably St Mawgan-in-Pydar
[2]—Probably St Stephen-in-Brannel

## to South Australia, MALES, by Occupation and Parish

| Labourer | Malster | Mason | Miller | Miner | Painter | Plasterer | Quarryman | Roper | Sawyer | Shepherd | Shoemaker | Tailor | Thatcher | Wheelwright | Totals |
|---|---|---|---|---|---|---|---|---|---|---|---|---|---|---|---|
| 2 | | | | | | | | | | | | | | | 3 |
| | | | | | | | | I | | | | | | | 2 |
| | | | | | | | | | | | I | | | 2 | 3 |
| | | | | | | | | | | | | | | | 2 |
| | | | | | | | | | | | | | | | I |
| | | | | | | | | | | | | | | | 2 |
| 2 | | | | | | | | | | | | | | | 5 |
| 2 | | I | | | | | | | | | | | | | 8 |
| | | | | | | | | | | | | | | | I |
| | | I | I | | | | | I | | | I | | | | 17 |
| 2 | | | | | | I | | | | | | | I | | 4 |
| | | | | | | | | | | | | | | | I |
| | | | | | | | I | | | | | | | | 2 |
| | | | | | | | | | | | | | | | I |
| 3 | | 3 | | | | | I | | | | | I | | | 9 |
| I | | 2 | | | | | | | | | | | | | 5 |
| | | | | | | | | | | | | | | | I |
| | | 2 | | | | | | | | | | | | | 3 |
| | | | | | | | | | | | | | | | 9 |
| I | | 2 | | | | | | | | | 3 | | | | 10 |
| 4 | | I | | | | | | | | | I | | | | 6 |
| | | | | | | | | | | I | | | | | I |
| | I | | | | | | | | | | | | | | I |
| 4 | | | | | | | | | | | | | | | 4 |
| | | | | | | | | | | | I | | | | I |
| | | | | 2 | | | | | | I | | | | | 6 |
| | | | | | | | | | | | | | | | I |
| | | | | | | | | | | | | | | | I |
| | | | | | | | | | | I | | | | | I |
| I | | | | | | | | | | | | | | | I |
| | | | | | | | | | | | | | | | 4 |
| | | I | | | | | | | | | | | | | 2 |
| | | 2 | | | | | | | | | | | | | 2 |
| | | | | | | | | | | | | | | | 3 |
| | | | | | | | | | | | | | | | 2 |
| | | | | | | | | | | | | | | | I |
| 2 | | I | | | | | I | | | | | | | | 6 |
| 5 | | | | | | | | | | | | | | | 6 |
| 29 | I | 16 | I | 2 | I | I | I | 2 | 2 | 2 | 7 | I | I | 2 | 138 |

Grand
Total

TABLE 4. 1839, Applications for Free Passage from Cornwall

| | Agricultural Labourer/Gardener | Accountant | Baker | Bellowmaker | Blacksmith | Builder | Butcher | Cabinet-maker | Cardwainer | Carpenter | Clerk | Carrier | Farmer/Husbandman | Harness-maker |
|---|---|---|---|---|---|---|---|---|---|---|---|---|---|---|
| Altarnun | 6 | | | | | | | | | 1 | | | | |
| Antony | 1 | | | | | | | | | | | | | |
| Bodmin | 5 | 1 | | | | | | | | | | | 2 | |
| Callington | | | | | | | | | | | | | | |
| Camelford | 1 | | | | | | | | | | | | | |
| Chacewater | 1 | | | | 2 | | | | | 1 | | | | |
| Creed | 1 | | | | | | | | | | | | | |
| Crowan | | | | | | | | | | | | | 1 | |
| Falmouth | 2 | | | | | | | | | 2 | 1 | | 2 | |
| Gerrans | 1 | | | | | | | | | | | | | |
| Gwennap | 5 | | | | | | 1 | | | 2 | | | | |
| Hayle | | | | | | | | | | | | | 1 | |
| Helston | | | | | 2 | | | | | | | | 1 | |
| Illogan | | | | | | | | | | 1 | | | 3 | |
| Jacobstowe | 1 | | | | | | | | | | | | | |
| Kenwyn | | | | | | | 1 | | | | | | 1 | |
| Laneast | | | | | | | | | | | | | | |
| Lanlivery | | | | | | | | | | | | | 2 | |
| Launceston | 1 | | | | | | 1 | | | | | | | |
| Lewannick | | | | | | | | | | | | | | |
| Linkinhorne | 1 | | | | | | | | | 1 | | | | |
| Liskeard | | | | | | | | | 1 | 2 | | | | |
| Lostwithiel | | | | | | | 1 | | | | | | | |
| Luxulyan | 1 | | | | | | | | | | | | | |
| Marazion | | | | | | | | | | | | | 2 | |
| Mylor | | | | | 1 | | | | | | | | | |
| North Hill | 1 | | | | | | | | | 1 | | | | |
| North Petherwin | | | | | | | | | | 1 | | | | |
| Padstow | 1 | | | | | | | | | | | | | |
| Paul | | | | | 3 | | | | | 2 | | | | |
| Penryn | 1 | | | | | 1 | | | | | | | | 1 |
| Penzance | 3 | | | | 1 | 1 | | 1 | | | | 1 | 7 | |
| Perranarworthal | | | | | | | | | | | | | | |
| Perranzabuloe | | | | | | | | | | | | | | |
| Probus | | | | | | | | | | | | | | |
| Redruth | | | 1 | 1 | | | 1 | | | | | | | |
| St Agnes | 5 | | | | | | | | 1 | 2 | | | | |
| St Austell | 1 | | | | | | | | | 1 | | | | |
| St Blazey | 7 | | | | 1 | | | | | | | | 1 | |

| Labourer | Mason | Miller | Millwright | Miner | Painter | Potter | Plumber | Quarry-worker | Sawyer | Shepherd | Shoemaker | Tailor | Tanner | Teacher | Wheelwright | Totals |
|---|---|---|---|---|---|---|---|---|---|---|---|---|---|---|---|---|
|  | 1 |  |  |  |  |  |  |  |  |  |  |  |  |  |  | 8 |
|  |  |  |  |  |  |  |  |  |  |  |  |  |  |  |  | 1 |
|  | 1 |  |  |  |  |  |  |  |  |  | 1 |  |  |  |  | 10 |
|  |  |  |  |  |  |  |  |  |  |  | 1 |  |  |  |  | 1 |
|  |  |  |  | 2 |  |  |  |  |  |  |  |  |  |  |  | 3 |
|  |  |  |  | 3 |  |  |  |  |  |  |  |  |  |  |  | 4 |
|  |  |  |  |  |  |  |  |  |  |  |  |  |  |  |  | 1 |
|  |  |  |  |  | 1 |  |  |  |  |  | 1 |  |  |  |  | 8 |
|  |  |  |  |  |  |  |  |  |  |  |  |  |  |  |  | 1 |
|  |  |  |  | 10 |  |  |  |  |  |  | 1 |  |  |  |  | 20 |
|  |  |  |  |  |  |  |  |  |  |  |  |  |  |  |  | 1 |
|  | 1 |  |  |  |  |  |  |  |  |  |  |  |  |  |  | 4 |
|  |  |  | 1 | 3 |  |  |  |  | 1 | 1 |  |  |  |  |  | 10 |
|  |  |  |  |  |  |  |  |  |  |  |  |  |  |  |  | 1 |
|  |  |  |  | 3 |  |  |  |  |  |  |  |  |  |  |  | 5 |
| 1 |  |  |  |  |  |  |  |  |  |  |  |  |  |  |  | 1 |
|  | 6 |  |  |  |  |  |  |  |  |  |  |  |  |  |  | 8 |
| 1 |  |  |  |  |  |  |  |  | 1 |  | 2 |  |  |  |  | 6 |
| 1 |  |  |  |  |  |  |  |  |  |  |  |  |  |  | 1 | 2 |
|  |  |  |  |  |  |  |  |  |  |  |  |  |  |  |  | 2 |
|  | 1 |  |  |  |  |  |  |  |  |  |  |  |  |  |  | 4 |
|  |  |  |  |  |  |  |  |  |  |  |  |  |  |  |  | 1 |
|  |  |  |  |  |  |  |  |  |  |  |  |  |  |  |  | 1 |
|  |  |  |  | 1 |  |  |  |  |  |  |  |  |  |  |  | 3 |
|  |  |  |  |  |  |  |  |  |  |  |  |  |  |  |  | 1 |
|  |  |  |  |  |  |  |  |  |  |  |  |  |  |  |  | 2 |
|  |  |  |  |  |  |  |  |  |  |  |  |  |  |  |  | 1 |
|  |  |  |  |  |  |  |  |  |  |  |  |  |  |  |  | 1 |
|  |  |  |  |  |  |  |  |  |  |  |  |  |  |  |  | 5 |
|  | 6 |  |  |  |  |  |  |  | 1 |  |  |  |  | 1 |  | 11 |
|  | 4 |  |  |  |  |  |  |  |  | 2 |  | 2 |  |  |  | 22 |
|  |  |  |  | 1 |  |  |  |  |  |  |  |  |  |  |  | 1 |
|  |  |  |  | 5 |  |  |  |  |  |  |  |  |  |  |  | 5 |
|  | 1 |  |  |  |  |  |  |  |  |  |  |  |  |  |  | 1 |
|  | 1 |  |  | 3 |  |  |  |  |  |  |  |  |  |  |  | 10 |
|  |  |  |  | 6 |  |  |  |  |  |  |  |  |  |  |  | 14 |
|  |  | 1 |  | 2 |  |  |  |  |  |  |  |  |  |  |  | 5 |
| 6 |  |  |  | 2 |  |  |  | 1 |  | 1 | 1 |  |  |  |  | 20 |

# TABLE 4. 1839, Applications for Free Passage from Cornwall

| | Agricultural Labourer/Gardener | Accountant | Baker | Bellowmaker | Blacksmith | Builder | Butcher | Cabinet-maker | Cardwainer | Carpenter | Clerk | Carrier | Farmer/Husbandman | Harness maker |
|---|---|---|---|---|---|---|---|---|---|---|---|---|---|---|
| St Breward | | | | | | | | | | | | | | |
| St Ewe | | | | | | 1 | | | | | | | 2 | |
| St Germans | | | | | | | | | | | | | | |
| St Goran | | | | | | | | | | | | | | |
| St Ives | 1 | | | | | | | | | 1 | | | | |
| St Keverne | | | | | | | | | | 1 | | | | |
| St Levan | | | | | | | | | | 1 | | | | |
| St Neot | | | | | 1 | | | | | | | | | |
| St Stephen¹ | 1 | | | | 1 | | | | | | | | | |
| St Thomas | | | | | | | | | | | | | | |
| South Petherwin | | | | | | | | | | | | | | |
| Stithians | | | | | | | 1 | | | | | | 1 | |
| Stoke Climsland | | | | | | | | | | 1 | | | | |
| Tregoney | 1 | | | | | | | | | | | | | |
| Truro | | | | | 2 | 1 | | | | 5 | | | 1 | |
| Tywardreath | 6 | | | | | | | | | | | | 1 | |
| Warleggan | 1 | | | | | | | | | | | | | |
| West Looe | | | | | | | | | | | 1 | | | |
| Unknown | 1 | | | | | | | | | | | | 1 | |
| **Totals** | 57 | 1 | 1 | 1 | 14 | 4 | 6 | 2 | 1 | 26 | 2 | 1 | 32 | 1 |

¹—Probably St Stephen-in-Brannel

## to South Australia, MALES, by Occupation and Parish

| Labourer | Mason | Miller | Millwright | Miner | Painter | Potter | Plumber | Quarry-worker | Sawyer | Shepherd | Shoemaker | Tailor | Tanner | Teacher | Wheelwright | Totals |
|---|---|---|---|---|---|---|---|---|---|---|---|---|---|---|---|---|
|  |  |  |  |  |  |  |  |  |  | 1 |  |  |  |  |  | 1 |
|  |  |  |  |  |  |  |  |  |  |  |  |  |  |  |  | 4 |
|  |  | 1 |  |  |  |  |  |  |  |  |  |  |  |  |  | 1 |
|  | 1 |  |  |  |  |  |  |  |  |  | 1 |  |  |  |  | 3 |
|  | 1 |  |  |  |  |  |  |  |  |  |  |  |  |  |  | 2 |
|  |  |  |  |  |  |  |  |  |  |  |  |  |  |  |  | 1 |
|  |  |  |  |  |  |  |  |  |  |  |  |  |  |  |  | 1 |
|  |  |  |  |  |  |  |  |  |  |  |  |  |  |  |  | 1 |
|  |  |  |  |  |  |  |  |  |  |  |  |  |  |  |  | 2 |
| 1 |  |  |  |  |  |  |  |  |  |  |  |  |  |  |  | 1 |
| 1 | 2 |  |  |  |  |  |  |  |  |  |  |  |  |  |  | 3 |
|  |  |  |  |  |  |  |  |  |  |  |  |  |  |  |  | 2 |
| 1 |  |  |  |  |  |  |  |  |  |  |  |  |  |  |  | 2 |
|  |  |  |  |  |  |  |  |  |  |  |  |  |  |  |  | 1 |
|  | 2 | 1 |  |  | 2 | 1 | 1 |  |  |  | 2 | 4 |  | 1 |  | 23 |
| 1 |  |  |  | 1 |  |  |  |  |  |  | 1 |  |  |  |  | 10 |
|  |  |  |  |  |  |  |  |  |  |  |  |  |  |  |  | 1 |
|  |  |  |  |  |  |  |  |  |  |  |  |  |  |  |  | 1 |
|  |  |  |  | 3 |  |  |  |  |  |  |  |  |  |  |  | 5 |
| 13 | 29 | 3 | 1 | 45 | 3 | 1 | 1 | 1 | 3 | 6 | 10 | 6 | 1 | 1 | 1 | 274 |

TABLE 5. 1840, Applications for Free Passage from Cornwall

| | Agricultural Labourer | Baker | Blacksmith | Butcher | Cabinet-maker | Carpenter | Carrier | Engineer | Farmer/Husbandman | Harness-maker | Labourer |
|---|---|---|---|---|---|---|---|---|---|---|---|
| Altarnun | 1 | | 1 | | | | | | | | 1 |
| Antony | | | | 1 | | 1 | | | | | |
| Callington | | | | | | | | | | | |
| Calstock | 1 | | | | | | | | | | |
| Camborne | | | 3 | | | | | | | | 1 |
| Camelford | | 2 | 1 | | | | | | | | |
| Chacewater | 1 | | | | | | | | 1 | | |
| Crowan | | | | | | | | | | | |
| Gerrans | | | | | | | | | 1 | | |
| Gwennap | | | | | | | | | | | 1 |
| Helston | | | | | | | | | 1 | | 1 |
| Illogan | | | | | | | | | 1 | | |
| Kea | 2 | | | | | | | | | | |
| Kenwyn | 1 | | | | | | | | | | |
| Launceston | 8 | | 1 | | 1 | | | | | | |
| Liskeard | 3 | | | | | | | | | | |
| Ludgvan | | | | | | 1 | | | | | |
| Mylor | | | | | | | | | 2 | | |
| Newlyn East | | | | | | | | | 1 | | |
| North Hill | | | | | | | | | | | |
| Penryn | | | | | | | | | 1 | | |
| Penzance | | | | | | | | | 1 | | |
| Perranarworthal | | | | | | | | | | | |
| Perranzabuloe | 1 | | | | | | | | | | 1 |
| Philleigh | | | | | | | | | | | 1 |
| Redruth | | | 2 | 1 | 1 | | | 1 | | | 1 |
| St Agnes | 1 | | 1 | | | | | 2 | | | 1 |
| St Allen | | | | | | | | | 1 | | |
| St Austell | | | | | | | | | | | |
| St Blazey | | | | | | | | | | | |
| St Clement | | | | | | 2 | | | | | |
| St Columb Major | 1 | | | | | | | | | | |
| St Eval | 1 | | | | | | | | | | |
| St Mawgan[1] | 1 | | | | | | | | | | |
| St Michael Caerhays | | | | | | | | | | | 1 |
| St Stephen-by -Launceston | | | | | | | | | | | |
| St Thomas | | | | | | | | | | | |
| Stithians | | | | | | | | | | | |
| Stoke Climsland | | | 1 | | | | | | | | |

| Malster | Mason | Miller | Miner | Ropemaker | Sawyer | Shepherd | Shoemaker | Tailor | Teacher | Tinman | Watchmaker | Wheelwright | Unknown | Totals |
|---|---|---|---|---|---|---|---|---|---|---|---|---|---|---|
| | | | | | | | | | | | | | | 3 |
| | | | | | | | | | | | | | | 2 |
| | | | | | | | | | | | | | | 1 |
| | | | 1 | | | | | | | | | | | 2 |
| | | | 18 | | 1 | | 2 | | | | | | 1 | 26 |
| | | | | | | | | | 1 | | | | | 4 |
| | | | 2 | | | | | | | | | | | 4 |
| | | 1 | | | | | | | | | | | | 1 |
| | | | | | | | | | | | | | | 1 |
| | | | 1 | | | | | | | | | | | 1 |
| | | 2 | 12 | | | | | | | | | | | 15 |
| | | | | | | | | | | | | | | 2 |
| | | | | | | | | | | | | | | 1 |
| | 1 | | 2 | | 1 | 1 | | | | 1 | | 1 | | 17 |
| | | | | | | | | | | | | | | 3 |
| | | | | | | | | | | | | | | 1 |
| | | | | | | | | | | | | | | 2 |
| | 1 | | | | | | | | | | | | | 2 |
| | | | | | | | | | | | | | | 1 |
| | | | | | | | | | | | 1 | | | 2 |
| | | | | | | | | | | | | | | 1 |
| | | 1 | | | | | | | | | | | | 1 |
| | | | 12 | | | | | | | | | | | 14 |
| | | | | | | | | | | | | | | 1 |
| 1 | | | 40 | | 3 | | | | | | | | | 50 |
| | | | 35 | | | | | | | | | | 1 | 41 |
| | | | | | | | | | | | | | | 1 |
| | | | | | 1 | | | | | | | | | 1 |
| | | 1 | | | | | | | | | | | | 1 |
| | | | | 1 | | | | | | | | | | 3 |
| | | 1 | | | 1 | | | | | | | 1 | | 4 |
| | | | | | | 1 | 1 | | | | | | | 3 |
| | | | | | | | | | | | | | | 1 |
| | | | | | 2 | | | | | | | | | 2 |
| | | | | | | | | | 1 | | | | | 1 |
| | | | | | 1 | | | | | | | | | 1 |
| | | | 9 | | | | | | | | | | | 10 |

## TABLE 5. 1840, Applications for Free Passage from Cornwall

| | Agricultural Labourer | Baker | Blacksmith | Butcher | Cabinet-maker | Carpenter | Carrier | Engineer | Farmer/Husbandman | Harness maker | Labourer |
|---|---|---|---|---|---|---|---|---|---|---|---|
| Talland | 1 | | | | | | | | | | |
| Truro | 3 | | | | | | | 1 | | 1 | |
| Veryan | | | 1 | | | | | | | | |
| Withiel | | | 1 | | | | | | | | |
| Unknown | | | | | | | | | | | |
| Totals | 27 | 2 | 12 | 2 | 2 | 4 | 1 | 3 | 10 | 1 | 9 |

¹—Probably St Mawgan-in-Pydar

## TABLE 6. Year Unknown (1836–40), Application for Free Passage from Cornwall to South Australia, MALES, by Occupation and Parish

| Parish | Mason | Farmer | Totals |
|---|---|---|---|
| St Keverne | — | 1 | 1 |
| Truro | 1 | — | 1 |
| TOTALS | 1 | 1 | 2 |

| Malster | Mason | Miller | Miner | Ropemaker | Sawyer | Shepherd | Shoemaker | Tailor | Teacher | Tinman | Watchmaker | Wheelwright | Unknown | Totals |
|---|---|---|---|---|---|---|---|---|---|---|---|---|---|---|
| | | | | | | | | | | | | | | 1 |
| | 1 | | | | | | 1 | | 1 | | | | | 8 |
| | | | | | | | 1 | 1 | | | | | | 3 |
| | | | | | | | | | | | | | | 1 |
| | | | | | | 1 | | | | | | | | 1 |
| 1 | 7 | 2 | 132 | 1 | 7 | 7 | 5 | 3 | 1 | 1 | 1 | 1 | 3 | 245 |

TABLE 7. 1837, Applications for Fre Passage from Cornwall to South Australia, SINGLE AND WIDOWED FEMALES, by Occupation and Parish

| Parish | Dairy-maid | Domestic Servant/ Servant | Farm Servant | Sempstress Dressmaker | Spinster | Totals |
|---|---|---|---|---|---|---|
| Callington | | 1 | | 1 | | 2 |
| Falmouth | | 1 | | | | 1 |
| Gwennap | | 3 | | 1 | | 4 |
| Illogan | | 1 | 1 | | | 2 |
| Launceston | | 1 | | 2 | | 3 |
| Linkinhorne | | 1 | | | | 1 |
| Mabe | | | | | 1 | 1 |
| Penryn | 1 | 1 | | 1 | | 3 |
| St Breward | 1 | 2 | | | | 3 |
| St Columb Major | | | 1 | | | 1 |
| Truro | | 1 | | | | 1 |
| Unknown | | 1 | | | | 1 |
| TOTALS | 2 | 13 | 2 | 5 | 1 | 23 |

TABLE 8. Applications for Free Passage from Cornwall to South Australia, SINGLE AND WIDOWED FEMALES, by Occupation and Parish

| | Dairymaid | Domestic Servant/ Servant | Farm Labourer's Widow | Farm Servant | Sempstress Dressmaker | Washerwoman | Unknown | Totals |
|---|---|---|---|---|---|---|---|---|
| Altarnun | 1 | 1 | | | | | | 2 |
| Bodmin | | | | | 2 | | | 2 |
| Crowan | 3 | | | | | | | 3 |
| Falmouth | | 1 | | | | | | 1 |
| Gwennap | | 2 | 1 | 2 | 3 | | | 8 |
| Launceston | | 5 | | | 1 | 1 | | 7 |
| Mevagissey | 1 | 12 | | | | | | |
| Mylor | | | | 1 | 1 | | | 2 |
| Perranarworthal | 1 | | | | | | | 1 |
| Perranzabuloe | 1 | | | | | | | 1 |
| Pillaton | | 1 | | 1 | | | | 2 |
| St Blazey | 1 | | | | | | 1 | 2 |
| Wendron | | | | | 1 | | | 1 |
| TOTALS | 8 | 11 | 1 | 4 | 8 | 1 | 1 | 34 |

TABLE 9. 1839, Applications for Free Passage from Cornwall to South Australia, SINGLE AND WIDOWED FEMALES, by Occupation and Parish

| | Confectioner | Dairymaid | Domestic Servant/ Servant | Farm Servant | Milliner/ Bonnet-maker | Sempstress/ Dressmaker | Shopmaid | Strawplaiter | Washerwoman | Widow | Totals |
|---|---|---|---|---|---|---|---|---|---|---|---|
| Altarnun | | 1 | | 2 | | | | | | | 3 |
| Bodmin | | 4 | 2 | | | 1 | | | | | 7 |
| Chacewater | | | 3 | | | | | | | | 3 |
| Crowan | | | 2 | | | 1 | | | | | 3 |
| Falmouth | | | | | 1 | 1 | | | | | 2 |
| Gwennap | | | 5 | 2 | | | | 1 | 1 | 1 | 10 |
| Helston | | 1 | | | 2 | 1 | | | | | 4 |
| Jacobstowe | | | 1 | | | | | | | | 1 |
| Kenwyn | | | 1 | | | | | | | | 1 |
| Landrake | | | | | | 1 | | | | | 1 |
| Linkinhorne | | | 3 | | | 1 | | | | | 4 |
| Lostwithiel | | | | | | 1 | | | | | 1 |
| North Hill | | 1 | | | | | | | | | 1 |
| Paul | | | 1 | | | | | | | | 1 |
| Penryn | | | 1 | 1 | | | | | | | 2 |
| Penzance | 2 | 1 | | | | 1 | | | | | 4 |
| Redruth | | | 2 | | | | | | | | 2 |
| St Agnes | | | 1 | | | 1 | | | | | 2 |
| St Austell | | | 1 | | | | | | | | 1 |
| St Blazey | | | 6 | | 1 | 1 | | | | | 8 |
| St Clether | | 1 | | | | | | | | | 1 |
| St Ewe | | | 2 | | | 2 | | | | | 4 |
| South Petherwin | | | | | | 1 | | | | | 1 |
| Stoke Climsland | | | 1 | | | | | | | | 1 |
| Truro | | | 1 | | 2 | 3 | | 1 | | | 7 |
| Tywardreath | | | 1 | | | | | | | | 1 |
| Unknown | | 2 | 1 | | | | 1 | | | | 4 |
| TOTALS | 2 | 11 | 35 | 5 | 6 | 16 | 1 | 2 | 1 | 1 | 80 |

131

TABLE 10. 1840, Applications for Free Passage to South Australia, SINGLE AND WIDOWED FEMALES, by Occupation and Parish

| | Balmaiden | Dairymaid | Domestic Servant/Servant | Farmer | Farm Servant | Homeduties | Milliner | "Plain Work" | Sempstress Dressmaker | Unknown | Totals |
|---|---|---|---|---|---|---|---|---|---|---|---|
| Callington | | | 1 | | | | | | | | 1 |
| Calstock | | | 1 | | | | | | | | 1 |
| Camborne | | | | | | | 1 | 1 | | 5 | 7 |
| Camelford | | | | | | | | 1 | | | 1 |
| Chacewater | | | | | | | | 1 | | | 1 |
| Falmouth | | | 1 | | | | | | | | 1 |
| Gwennap | | | 1 | | | | | | | | 1 |
| Helston | | | | | | | | | 1 | | 1 |
| Illogan | | | 2 | | | | | | | | 2 |
| Kea | | | 1 | 1 | | | | | | | 2 |
| Launceston | | 1 | 1 | | | | | | | | 2 |
| Perranarworthal | | | 1 | | | | | | | | 1 |
| Perranzabuloe | | | 1 | | | | | | | | 1 |
| Philleigh | | | 1 | | | | | | | | 1 |
| Redruth | | 1 | 12 | | | 1 | | | | 2 | 16 |
| St Agnes | 2 | 5 | 1 | | | | 2 | | 1 | 1 | 12 |
| St Columb Major | | 2 | | | | | | | 1 | | 3 |
| St Eval | | | 1 | | | | | | | | 1 |
| St Pinnock | | 1 | | | | | | | | | 1 |
| Stoke Climsland | | | 1 | | | | | | | | 1 |
| Truro | | | 1 | | | | | | | | 1 |
| Veryan | | | 1 | | 1 | | | | | | 2 |
| Unknown | | | | | | | | | | 1 | 1 |
| TOTALS | 2 | 10 | 28 | 1 | 1 | 1 | 2 | 1 | 6 | 9 | 61 |

# APPENDIX 4

ANALYSIS OF OCCUPATIONS OF ADULT CORNISH IMMIGRANTS INTO SOUTH AUSTRALIA, 1848–67, FOR WHOM OCCUPATIONS ARE RECORDED, ALSO SHOWING PERCENTAGE OF MINERS AMONGST MALE CORNISH IMMIGRANTS IN EACH YEAR (2 TABLES)

*Source: S.A.A. 313 Passenger Lists.*

TABLE 1. Adult Male Cornish Immigrants into South Australia for whom occupations are recorded, 1848–67

| Year | Agricultural Labourer | Baker | Blacksmith | Carpenter | Cooper | Engineer | Farmer | Labourer | Mariner | Mason | Miller | Miner | Painter | Police Constable | Quarryman | Sawyer | School-master | Shepherd | Shoemaker | Weaver | Wheelwright | Total per year | Miners % |
|---|---|---|---|---|---|---|---|---|---|---|---|---|---|---|---|---|---|---|---|---|---|---|---|
| 1848 | 17 | | 2 | 1 | | | | 1 | | 1 | | 5 | | | | 1 | | | | | 1 | 28 | 17.9 |
| 1849 | 63 | | 4 | 4 | | | 2 | 11 | | 2 | | 27 | | | | | | | | | | 114 | 23.7 |
| 1850 | 18 | | | | | | 1 | 30 | 1 | 3 | | 12 | | | | | | | | | 1 | 69 | 8.3 |
| 1851 | 43 | | 1 | 2 | | 2 | | 14 | | 4 | | 130 | 1 | | | | | | 3 | | | 194 | 67.0 |
| 1852 | 47 | 1 | 5 | 2 | | | 1 | 3 | | 1 | | 28 | | | | | | | | | | 83 | 33.7 |
| 1853 | 25 | | 5 | 6 | 1 | | | 8 | | | | 66 | | | | | 1 | 2 | 4 | | | 117 | 56.4 |
| 1854 | 22 | | 8 | 7 | | | | 35 | | 9 | | 187 | | | | | | | 2 | | | 275 | 68.0 |
| 1855 | 4 | | 6 | 4 | | | | 27 | | 6 | | 180 | | | | 2 | | | | | | 230 | 78.3 |
| 1856 | 38 | | 5 | 4 | | | | 24 | | 3 | | 200 | | | 1 | 1 | | 2 | 1 | | | 277 | 72.2 |
| 1857 | 28 | | | | | | | 24 | | 1 | | 444 | | | 3 | 1 | | | | 1 | | 501 | 88.6 |
| 1858 | 25 | | 1 | | | | | 23 | | | | 126 | | | 1 | | | | 1 | | | 178 | 70.8 |
| 1859 | 5 | | 1 | | | | | 7 | | | | 4 | | | | | | | | | | 18 | 22.2 |
| 1860 | 6 | | 1 | | | | | 3 | | | | 22 | | | | | | | 1 | | | 33 | 66.7 |
| 1861 | | | | | | | | | | | | | | | | | | | | | | 0 | — |
| 1862 | 1 | | 3 | | | | 1 | 12 | | 1 | | 56 | | | | 1 | | | | | | 86 | 65.1 |
| 1863 | 8 | | 3 | 3 | | | 1 | 51 | | | | 120 | | | | 1 | | | 1 | | 4 | 194 | 61.9 |
| 1864 | 3 | | 40 | 23 | | 7 | 3 | 233 | | 35 | | 132 | 1 | 1 | 1 | 10 | | | 7 | | 5 | 510 | 25.9 |
| 1865 | 9 | | | 7 | 1 | 2 | | 65 | 1 | 4 | 1 | 46 | 1 | | 2 | 4 | | | | | 1 | 144 | 32.0 |
| 1866 | 3 | | 9 | 4 | | | | 10 | | 2 | | 12 | | | | | | | 3 | | | 72 | 16.7 |
| 1867 | 42 | | 1 | 3 | | | | | | 2 | | | | | | | | 2 | | | | 50 | 0 |
| Totals | 407 | 1 | 91 | 70 | 2 | 11 | 9 | 581 | 2 | 72 | 1 | 1797 | 3 | 1 | 8 | 24 | 1 | 6 | 24 | 1 | 12 | 3124 | 57.5 |

TABLE 2. Adult Female Cornish Immigrants into South Australia for whom Occupations are Recorded, 1848–67

| Year | Balmaiden | Domestic Servant | Female Cook | Female Farm Servant | Laundress | Milliner | Nurse | Sempstress | Total per year |
|---|---|---|---|---|---|---|---|---|---|
| 1848 | | 6 | | 1 | | | | 1 | 8 |
| 1849 | | 45 | | | 1 | | | 2 | 48 |
| 1850 | | 37 | | 1 | | | | | 38 |
| 1851 | 2 | 57 | | 1 | | | | 2 | 62 |
| 1852 | | 21 | | 6 | | | | | 27 |
| 1853 | 3 | 30 | | 2 | | 1 | 2 | 1 | 39 |
| 1854 | | 70 | | 6 | | | | 4 | 80 |
| 1855 | | 46 | | | | | | | 46 |
| 1856 | | 31 | | | | | | | 31 |
| 1857 | | 56 | | | | | | | 56 |
| 1858 | | 40 | 1 | | | | | 3 | 44 |
| 1859 | | 20 | | | | | | | 20 |
| 1860 | | 20 | | | | | | | 20 |
| 1861 | | | | | | | | | 0 |
| 1862 | | 1 | | | | | | | 1 |
| 1863 | | 13 | | | | | | | 13 |
| 1864 | | 50 | | | | | | | 50 |
| 1865 | | 143 | | | | | 1 | 1 | 145 |
| 1866 | | 45 | | | | | | | 45 |
| 1867 | | 24 | | | | | | 2 | 26 |
| TOTALS | 5 | 755 | 1 | 17 | 1 | 1 | 3 | 16 | 799 |

# APPENDIX 5

## INDEX OF CORNISH EMIGRANT FAMILIES

Abrahams 79; Allen 31, 55, 64, 101; Andrew 84; Angove 33; Angwin 34; Arnall 16; Arthur 98; Axford 87, 97; Badge 72; Barbary 85; Barrett 34; Bartlett 59; Bassett 64; Bastian 54, 55, 98; Bawden 78, 83; Beaglehole 79; Bennetts 11; Berryman 20; Best 17, 27, 54; Bettess 84, 88; Binney 53, 98; Blight 72, 75; Boaden 19; Bone 72, 73; Bonython 16, 35–41, 106; Borlace 84; Bossnall 16; Boucaut 22, 39, 41, 47, 48, 83, 91, 92, 106; Bowden 15, 52, 77, 85, 94; Bray 15, 43, 70, 72, 74, 79; Broad 33; Brock 79; Brokenshire 44; Bryant 23, 94, 95, 98; Bull 49; Buzzacott 72; Carbis 20; Carne 14; Carlyon 34; Carter 98, 99; Chenoweth 86; Champion 13, 17; Chapman 73, 74; Chappell 78, 84; Christopher 75; Cobbledick 54, 55; Cock 85; Cocking 15; Colliver 84; Colwill 57; Cook 97; Coombe 31, 43; Cornelius 14, 55; Corner 15; Cornish 30, 56; Coumbe 35; Courtis 65; Cowling 79; Crewes 71; Curnow 38, 72; Daddow 85; Daniels 87; Davey 28; Davies 53; Dawe 55; Dennis 59; Dingle 99, 100; Dinham 30; Dungey 32; Dunn 27, 30, 81; Dunstan 16, 28, 34, 71, 73, 90, 95, 96, 98; Dunstone 31, 73; Edgecombe 59; Edwards 31; Edyvean 84; Ellery 98; Ellis 86; Escott 71; Fradd 71; Ford 84; Fry 43; Gartrell 59; Gill 88; Glasson 59, 72, 97; Goldsworthy 78; Goodman 57; Gray 14, 72; Grenfell 11; Grey 75; Grose 35; Grylls 31; Guy 64; Harme 12; Hammer 20, 33; Hancock 21; Harris 55, 64, 69, 72, 79, 98; Harry 43; Harvey 17, 30, 31, 58; Hawke 59, 70; Hawker 59; Hender 49, 53; Herring 55; Hick 59; Hicks 17; Hill 98; Hilman 49; Hocking 79; Holman 28, 56; Hooper 86; Hosking 97, 99; Hoskyn 14; Jacka 98; Jacobs 53; Jagoe 39; James 32, 33, 79, 100, 101; Jenkin 84, 101; Jenkins 71; Jennings 97; Jewell 57, 79; Johns 57; Jones 35, 64; Kemp 20; Kernick 54, 55; King 32, 84; Lander 77; Langdon 87; Laurimer 12, 13, 14, 30; Lawry 79; Leane 59; Leggoe 101; Liddicoat 80, 84; Madden 79; Magor 45, 57, 59; Major 79, 94; Male 54, 55; Mallett 13; Manuel 84; Marks 20; Martin 27, 54, 60–62, 64, 80, 95, 98, 107; Matthews 59; May 64, 79, 80; Mayne 86; Medland 49; Menhennet 97; Mildren 64; Mitchell 59, 71, 72; Montgomery 13; Morcombe 75; Moyle 38, 72, 94, 99; Moyses 72, 74, 75; Mutton 80; Nankervis 70, 81; Nankivell 83; Nicholls 55, 98; Ninnes 73; Northey 98; Nottle 59, 98, 99; Nunan 95; Oates 79; Oliver 70; Opie 21, 96; Orchard 19, 53; Organ 13, 14; Osborne 33, 35; Painter 38; Parsons 35, 36, 45; Pascoe 39, 69; Paul 14, 75; Paull 79; Paynter 20, 99, 100; Pearce 55, 70, 72; Pedler 28, 58; Penaluna 34; Pengilly 26, 53, 95; Penrose 75, 100; Pethick 53; Philips 20; Phillips 26, 33, 79, 83; Philp 59; Pierce 28; Pillern 20; Pinch 72; Polglase 98; Polkinghorne 54, 55, 86; Pollard 79; Pomeroy 99; Prideaux 34; Prior 45, 72; Prisk 88; Prowse 84; Pryor 72, 75; Quick 20; Quintrell 84; Rendell 49; Reseigh 45; Richards 12, 20, 55, 73, 99; Roach 70, 72, 84, 97; Roberts 57, 97; Robins 12, 13, 14, 72; Rodda 80, 83, 84, 88; Rose 85; Rosewarne 81; Rounsevell 35–38, 41, 91; Rowe 43, 49, 50, 57, 64, 88, 104; Rule 70, 86; Rundle 49; Sampson 55, 56, 72, 94; Sanders 31, 55, 56, 97; Sando 80; Sandow 73, 75; Santo 18, 31, 44, 47; Sara 53, 55, 71; Saunders 20; Sawle 29, 30, 43, 46, 51; Scoble 84; Scown 14; Secomb 59; Short 45, 64; Sibley 95; Sibly 55; Skewes 57, 59, 94; Sleep 14, 28, 73; Sloggatt 30; Smith 16; Stanton 16; Stephens 7, 8, 10,

23, 43, 45, 46, 59, 84, 86, 106; Stevens 38; Stocker 21; Symonds 59; Symons 79, 86; Taylor 20; Teague 20, 73, 98, 101; Temby 59; Thomas 55, 71, 72, 84, 94, 97; Tiddy 79; Tippett 51; Tonkin 49, 56, 80; Treais 21; Tregea 16; Tregoweth 88; Trelaggan 75; Trelease 79; Treleaven 65, 72, 74, 97, 99; Treloar 71, 103; Trelour 20; Tremain 56; Trembath 70; Tremelling 45; Trenaman 55; Trengove 84, 88; Trenouth 49, 50, 56; Tresise 97; Tresize 85; Trestrail 51; Trethowan 85; Trevail 45; Trevena 20, 72, 97; Trevorrow 101; Trewin 99; Trewren 75; Trezona 78; Trudgen 34, 107; Turner 52, 70, 71; Uren 20; Vanstone 55; Varcoe 59; Veal 87; Vellanoweth 53, 54; Venning 17, 49, 53; Verco 30, 44, 47; Wait 71; Waterhouse 46; Waters 55, 69, 98, 99; Wearne 87; Webb 75; Whitburn 79; Williams 23, 54, 55, 72, 78, 87, 98, 99; Wills 60, 97; Wincey 64, 65; Worden 58; Worth 21; Yeoman 100.

# General Index

*Cornish Carols From Australia*

Dr Payton has rediscovered a nineteenth-century collection of Cornish Carols, first published in the South Australian copper-mining town of Moonta in 1893. In his introduction, Dr Payton explains the Carols' significance as parts of both the Cornish musical tradition and Cornwall's "Great Migration".

ISBN 0 907566 92 8                    Card Covers £2.50

". . . . a book that will arouse joyous chords of welcome . . . Dr Payton and his publishers are to be commended for arranging this republication of something which must rank high in value in the musical heritage and traditions of the Cornish people."

Dr John Rowe in the *Cornish Banner*